Contents

AF729004

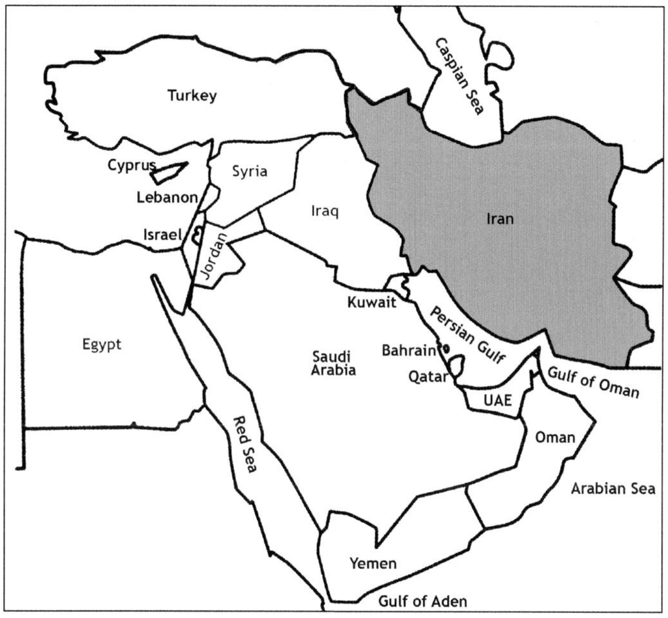

Helion & Company Limited
Unit 8 Amherst Business Centre, Budbrooke Road, Warwick CV34 5WE, England
Tel. 01926 499 619
Email: info@helion.co.uk Website: www.helion.co.uk Twitter: @helionbooks Visit our blog http://blog.helion.co.uk/

Published by Helion & Company 2026
Designed and typeset by Mach 3 Solutions (www.mach3solutions.co.uk)
Cover designed by Paul Hewitt, Battlefield Design (www.battlefield-design.co.uk)

Text © Leon Manouchehrians with Sander Peeters 2026
Colour artworks & maps drawn by and © Leon Manouchehrians 2026

Front cover: Two Persian Air Army Corps Hornet-powered Hawker Audaxes conduct an attack on the camp of Baluch tribe separatists in the province of Baluchestan and Sistan during the Persian Civil War of the 1930s. The foreground aircraft is 213, one of the early Audax deliveries with an American Pratt and Whitney engine. Hawker Audaxes were armed with bombs underwing and machine guns in the rear cockpit. (Artwork by Renato Dalmaso © Helion & Company 2026)

Every reasonable effort has been made to trace copyright holders and to obtain their permission for the use of copyright material. The author and publisher apologise for any errors or omissions in this work, and would be grateful if notified of any corrections that should be incorporated in future reprints or editions of this book.

ISBN 978-1-806720-25-5

British Library Cataloguing-in-Publication Data.
A catalogue record for this book is available from the British Library.

All rights reserved. No part of this publication may be reproduced, stored in a retrieval system, or transmitted, in any form, or by any means, electronic, mechanical, photocopying, recording or otherwise, without the express written consent of Helion & Company Limited.

For details of other military history titles published by Helion & Company Limited contact the above address, or visit our website: http://www.helion.co.uk. We always welcome receiving book proposals from prospective authors.

ABBREVIATIONS & ACRONYMS

AELR	*Air & Espace – Lucht-en Ruimtevaart* (Brussels Air Museum, Belgium)
AKTA	*Az Keykavoos ta Aryamehr* (from Keykavoos to Aryamehr)
AIOC	Anglo-Iranian Oil Company
APOC	Anglo-Persian Oil Company, renamed AIOC in 1935
c/n	construction number
DBR	damaged beyond repair
DLH	*Deutsche Lufthansa* (German national airline company)
GVF	Civil Air Fleet (Armenian)
hp	horsepower
IIAF	Imperial Iranian Air Force (official name of air force from 1935 until 1979)
INA	Iran National Archive
JLP	*Junkers Luftverkehr Persien* (Junkers Air Transport Persia)
JLR	*Junkers Luftverkehr Russland* (Junkers Air Transport Russia)
kph	kilometres per hour
kW	kilowatt
mph	miles per hour
msn	manufacturer's serial number
NIOC	National Iranian Oil Company
OTU	Operational Training Unit
PAAC	Persian Army Air Corps (official name of the Iranian air force until 1935)
PTT	Post, Telegram & Telephone (national mail company of Persia, later Iran)
qty	quantity
RAF	Royal Air Force (United Kingdom)
rpm	rotations per minute
SPAD	*Société Pour L'Aviation et ses Dérivés*
UK	United Kingdom
US(A)	United States (of America)
USAAF	United States Army Air Force
USSR	Union of Soviet Socialist Republics
VVS	*Voenno-Vozdushnye Sily* (Military Air Force) – Soviet Air Force
VVS RKKA	Air Force of the Workers-Peasants of the Red Army

ACKNOWLEDGEMENTS

The author wishes to extend heartfelt gratitude to the following individuals and organisations for their invaluable support, contributions, and encouragement. These are, in alphabetical order, listed below:

Abbas Atrvash, Babak Taghvaee, Behruz Atayee, Fereydoon Behmanesh, Fred Nassirkhani, Kaveh Farrokh, Lennart Anderson, Marcel Kares, Matofi, Mehdi Khosravinejad, Mirpanj, Paul van den Elsaker, Phil Guston, Pizo Ortega-SNA, Sander Peeters, Stewart/AB-IX, Stuart-DH Moth Club, Sohrab Riahi and Tom Cooper.

Above all, the author is deeply indebted to his wife, Rima, and his daughter, Natalie. Without their unwavering support, patience, and sacrifice, the completion of this book would not have been possible.

PREFACE

Growing up in Iran, it was natural that my passion for aviation evolved into a deep interest in the country's civil and military aviation. Yet, the more I searched for information, the more I discovered the near-total absence of reliable archives or published material. Researching Iran's aviation history – civil or military – was nearly impossible. Civil documents and photos were scarce, and on the military side, a culture of secrecy meant that anyone asking questions or holding a camera was viewed as a potential spy. Reliable sources felt as rare as a buried treasure.

My first real opportunity came in the late 1960s, when articles I published in *Iranian Skies*, the monthly journal of the Imperial Aero Club, led to an invitation to volunteer with the Imperial Iranian Air Force publishing department. There, I had access to non-classified documents and photo archives with Class-3 clearance.

After moving to the United States in 1978, just before the Islamic Revolution, I began compiling and digitising my documents and photographs, while continuing to follow the decline of Iranian aviation from its pre-revolutionary peak to its later struggles. The lack of comprehensive sources on Iran's aviation history – particularly on its military power – posed a serious risk of erasing knowledge for future generations. That sense of urgency drove me to share my 50 years of collected archives.

In 2010, I launched the *Iranian Aviation Review*, the first and only English-language magazine dedicated to Iran's civil and military aviation. The publication received strong support from aviation enthusiasts worldwide. Still, I believed a book – lasting and accessible to a broader audience – would leave a greater mark. With *Iranian Air Power* as part of the *Middle East@War Series* by Helion, my goal is to introduce readers to the remarkable yet little-known history of one of the world's most overlooked air forces.

Leon Manouchehrians,
Glendale, CA, USA,
October 2025

1

ON THE PATH TO PROGRESS

Iran, known as Persia from ancient history, is located in the centre of the Middle East. With 1,648,195km^2 (636,372 square miles) of territory, it borders with Armenia, Azerbaijan and Turkmenistan in the north, Afghanistan and Pakistan in the east, and Turkey and Iraq in the west. It has coasts on the Caspian Sea in the north and the Persian Gulf and Sea of Oman in the south. The warm waters of the latter provide direct access around the world via the Indian Ocean.

From ancient times, Persia possessed a strong army and navy. It has been considered as one of the world's major military powers with major victories against the Romans, Ottomans, Greeks and Arabs. The armed forces, however, went into a steady decline starting in medieval times until the nineteenth century.

During the First World War, the Qajar dynasty ruled Persia. The federal government was weak, unorganised and corrupt. While the Qajar kings were spending national wealth on their year-round lavish lifestyle in European countries, most of Persia's population lived in poverty.

Backed by foreign influence, tribal uprisings were widespread. Several armed tribes established autonomous governments in different parts of the country and declared independence from the federal government. A civil war was on the horizon in the country. It was obvious that without a strong leader and modern army, Persia could never maintain its sovereignty.

Persian Colonel Reza Khan, an officer from the highly disciplined Cossack Cavalry Division of the Persian Army, was a true nationalist. Vigorous and unrelenting on forgiving mistakes, he overthrew the Qajar-appointed government in a bloodless coup d'état in 1921 and established a military government, becoming commander-in-chief of the Army and minister of war.

Reza Shah Pahlavi. (Historica Fandom)

On 26 October 1923, Reza Khan was appointed as prime minister by Ahmad Shah, the last king of the Qajar dynasty, while he was vacationing in France. This provided the opportunity and power Reza Khan needed in the *Majlis* (the Iranian Parliament) to rule the country as he saw fit. On 14 December 1925, the *Majlis* abolished the Qajar dynasty and announced the establishment of the *Pahlavi* dynasty.

On 15 December 1925, after a high-profile coronation ceremony, Reza Khan became the first king of Pahlavi, dubbed His Imperial Majesty Reza Shah Pahlavi the Great (*Reza Shah-e-Kabir*). Reza Shah was a visionary man ahead of his time. His goal was to transform Persia from an agricultural third world nation to a modern industrial country.

With the proven effectiveness of air power during the First World War, the Iranian government was interested in establishing their own air force to support the Army. A first attempt was made in June 1919, when the Persian government approached the United Kingdom and requested aircraft for its newly established Gendarmerie from the RAF (Royal Air Force) inventory in Mesopotamia (current-day Iraq). As Britain had no intention to strengthen the Persian military and police forces, the request was rejected.

In 1922, Reza Khan, as a commander-in-chief of the Persian army, ordered for an 'air office' to be established at the Army's headquarters and appointed Army Colonel Mizrani as the director of the Army Air Corps. This was the beginning of military aviation in Iran. The Persian Army Air Corps (PAAC), as it was called, became an integral part of the Army and was under its direct command.

That same year, the Persian State Department approached the United States for aircraft, training, and technical support. The United States, however, was hosting the International Conference on Disarmament and believed that military aid was not in line with its foreign policy and thus the request was refused. Iran turned to other major powers of the time, including Germany, France and the Soviet Union.

France and the Soviet Union offered limited training and tied the sale of small quantities of aircraft and ammunition to oil concessions. Germany, on the other hand, wasted no time in recognising Iran's

Early crest of PAAC included an eagle with spread wings flying under the Imperial crown. (Leon Manouchehrians)

potential for air transport in a country that had a few railways, an inadequate road system and two mountain ranges bordering the central plateau.

THE PERSIAN JUNKERS COMPANY

By 1923, some of the non-military restrictions imposed by the Treaty of Versailles on Germany had already been eased. This allowed *Junkers-Luftverkehr Gmbh*, a pioneer in manufacturing all-metal transport aircraft for civilian use, to approach the Persian government on its plans to start an air service on the Stockholm-Moscow-Tehran route. Junkers' representative Jaroljmek was granted a meeting with Reza Khan.

On 14 May 1923, Junkers sent an F 13 (R-RECA) all-metal transport to Tehran for demonstration purposes. The aircraft was joined by a second F 13 (R-RECI) two days later, and a third (R-RECC) four days after. The three aircraft made several flights over the capital and stayed in Persia for two weeks, making demonstration flights and taking government officials for their first airplane ride as well. Joyrides were also given to high-ranking military officers, such as Lieutenant General Rahim Amirbeygi (Commander of the Central Division) and Major General Ebrahim Afghami (Commander of the Army Artillery Brigade), both of whom later recommended the Shah to order and use the Junkers aircraft in military operations against rebellious tribes.

R-RECC flew on to Isfahan, Tabriz, Hamadan and Mashhad and made propaganda flights carrying Persian officials. Local people also came to see the 'metal bird', which was the first time most of them had seen an airplane up close. The overall attempt by Junkers to impress influential officials proved to be successful. Their favourable view towards Junkers' activities in Persia paved the way for their involvement in planning and shaping of the Persian air transportation system for the next decade.

The Junkers Company proposed to provide aircraft, crew training and technical support, as well as establishing pilot training and mechanic schools to train Iranians in those roles. The company also pledged to construct maintenance facilities, new airfields and provide flight safety by installing adequate radio communication equipment, beacons, transmitters and other navigational facilities.

At the time, Tehran's only airfield was Ghaleh Morghi (Farsi for bird nest), an open area located some three miles south of the capital, flattened by the British government to be used as a refuelling stop by RAF aircraft en route from Iraq to India.

Persian officers visiting the first F 13 (R-RECA) that arrived at Ghaleh Morghi airfield. German pilot Jüeterbock is sitting on the edge of the open cockpit. The man with the hat and raincoat standing in front is the German envoy to Persia. (INA)

Junkers F 13 R-RECI performing demonstration flights over Tehran with Persian officials onboard. (Dmitri Kessel)

On foot or by donkey... people came to see the metal bird up close. The man with the white robe on the left is the *Kadkhoda* or the head of the village adjacent to the airfield. (Iran-e-Ghadim)

An F 13 under maintenance at the first hangar erected by Junkers at Ghaleh Morghi. (INA)

Bird's eye view of Ghaleh Morghi airfield as it stood with two hangars and a central administration building in 1927. Note the parked Junkers F 13s and curved aircraft tracks on the unpaved ground. (Iran-e-Ghadim)

Junkers' efforts paid off and their offer was accepted. What influenced the Shah's choice was that he had a passion for discipline, something in line with his pro-German sentiment, and a personal dislike of the British and distrust of the Soviets. The Shah even agreed to subsidise the purchase. Subsequently, the Iranian Junkers company JLP (*Junkers Luftverkehr Persien*) was established in April 1924 as a subsidiary of the German *Junkers Flugzeugwerke*.

Between May 1924 and August 1927, Junkers transferred five Polikarpov PS-2 aircraft to Tehran under a five-year wet-lease contract.[1] All five PS-2s were ex-JLR (*Junkers Luftverkehr Russland*, Junkers Air Transport Company Russia) aircraft. Four more Junkers F 13s were also supplied directly from Junkers' Dessau plant in Germany.[2]

In anticipation of their use in military operations, the Persian Ministry of War requested that two of the German-assembled F 13s (D-703 and D-704) be fitted in Moscow with non-standard machine gun stands on the roof of the cabin before delivery to Persia. However, no weapons were to be supplied with the aircraft, since documents identified them as civil transport aircraft. Two other aircraft (R-RECE and R-RECG) were floatplanes that were earmarked for use between the Caspian Sea ports of Anzali, Gazz and Astara with Baku in the Soviet Republic of Azerbaijan. The floats could be replaced with landing gear by four men in about three hours, allowing them to be used on regular routes as well, should the need arise.

Local peasants visit an F 13 at Boushehr. This photograph clearly shows the difficulties and challenges Junkers personnel must have endured operating in an underdeveloped, rural country in the 1920s. (Will Grothe collection)

On 1 October 1924, Junkers was granted a biweekly service on the Tehran-Anzali-Baku route. The new air service started immediately with four-passenger F 13 floatplanes. Junkers erected a maintenance hangar at Tehran and floating docks for seaplanes at Anzali, next to the newly established naval facilities. From Baku, a Soviet-based Junkers subsidiary flew on to Moscow via Mineralye Vode, Rostov and Kharkov. Connection from Moscow to Berlin was provided by the Soviet-German airline *Deruluft* (*Deutsch-Russische Luftverkehrs AG*), which later came to be known as *Interflug*, the official airline of East Germany after the Second World War.

Table 1: Junkers F 13s of the *Junkers Luftverkehr Persien*

Type	Registration	c/n	Name	Delivered	Notes
PS-2	R-RECK	569	*Sehre* (Finch)	1924	Renamed *Gilan* by PAAC. To Lufthansa as D-650, later D-1183
PS-2	R-RECE	614	*Khoroos* (Rooster)	1924	Used mostly as a floatplane. Scrapped in Shiraz as source of parts
PS-2	R-RECC	643	*Kalagh* (Crow)	1924	Civil transport, to PAAC as No 25. To Lufthansa as D-766, later D-231
PS-2	R-RECI	651	*Tavoos* (Peacock)	1925	Civil transport, to PAAC as No 26. Suffered ground fire damage in Yazd, 1930
PS-2	R-RECG	693	*Morgh* (Hen)	1926	Floatplane, to PAAC as No 24. Suffered ground fire damage in Yazd, 1930
F 13a	D-703	675	*Joojeh* (Chicken)	1925	Rooftop machine gun stand, No 23. Stored Tehran 1928, scrapped 1930
F 13a	D-704	676	*Kabk* (Partridge)	1925	Rooftop machine gun stand, No 27. DBR, and grounded, Boushehr 1929
F 13f	D-1071	800	*Morghabi* (Teal)	1926	Renamed *Simorgh* by PAAC. To Lares Romania as CV-JAC
F 13f	D-1126	2001	*Karkas* (Vulture)	1927	Leased to Anglo-Persian Oil Co. Returned to Junkers as D-OHAS

Cossack cavalry and Army soldiers guard the two Dessau-built F 13s fitted with rooftop machine gun positions, albeit without any machine gun installed. Note the two German pilots standing on the aircraft at left. (artiklar.z-bok.se)

Thus, it was theoretically possible to fly from London or any other Western capital via Berlin and Moscow to Tehran by a largely German airline system. However, it was not long before the Soviet government restricted air transport in the Soviet Union to its own airline, *Ukrwosduchputj* (which later became *Aeroflot*), which took over responsibility of flights on the route from Moscow to Baku and Tbilisi from Junkers.

The route from Konigsberg to Moscow had never been served by Junkers as *Deruluft* had the exclusive rights to that route. On 26 January 1926, *Junkers Luftverkehr* of Germany was integrated into *Deutsche Lufthansa AG* (DLH) and all Junkers air transport activities were stopped.

However, the Persian subsidiary continued to operate separately, and Junkers representative Kurt Weil was sent to Tehran for the management of the air transportation venture. Junkers concentrated on the final part of the route in Persia, and on 8 February 1927, a regular service between Tehran and Kermanshah and Hamadan on the Iraqi border was inaugurated. This was followed in April 1928 by a new route from Tehran to Boushehr on the Persian Gulf via Isfahan and Shiraz and later other routes to Mashhad in 1929 and Tabriz via Qazvin in 1930.

The Persian Junkers Company flew a weekly postal and passenger service between Tehran and the centre of the provinces. Aside from

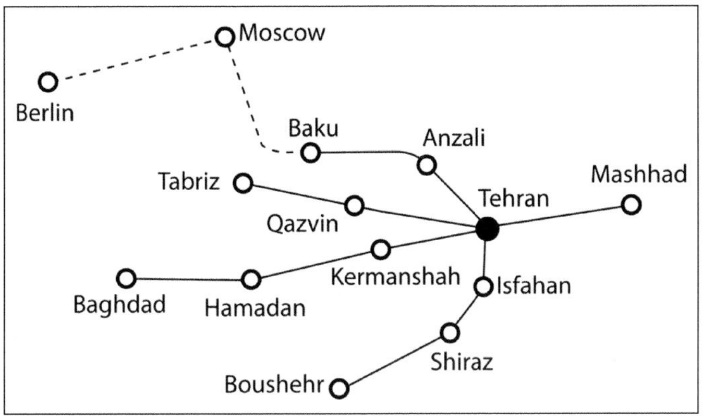

A schematic of the route network of the Persian Junkers Company in 1930. (Leon Manouchehrians)

Table 2: German pilots and mechanics of JLP

Name	Notes
Achilles, Paul	Started to fly for JLP 20 April 1929
Bauerhin, Kurt	Hired 1925, was active in combat until 1928
Guenther, Werner	With JLP since 1928, died when with LAB, 1932
Haal, Erich	Flew for JLP 1929–1930
Haenichen, Martin	Flew for JLP 1929–1930, 1931 to South America
Harder, Fritz	Flew for JLP in 1931
Hesse, Hans	Flew for JLP 1923–1926, to DLH 1926
Jüeterbock, Georg	Flew for JLP 1924–31, died Bolivia 1940
Kudryavstev, Peter	Flew for JLP 1928, killed 1938 in LAB crash
Messbaucher, Robert	Flew for JLP 1925–1927, crashed 1931
Schaefer, Othello	Flew for JLP 1924–1927, left Junkers 1928
Wagner, Peter	Died in Tehran 1927, details unknown
Wasserthal, Walter	Flew for JLP in 1924, suicide in port of Pahlevi
Wangenheim, Stams	Died in a crash at Dresden, Germany, 1938
Taumann, Morzik	Served in JLP as pilot/mechanic 1924–1929

Broujerd, Persia, 1925. Members of the Cossack cavalry of the Persian army standing on guard to protect a PAAC Junkers F 13. The man on the horse is Robert Messbaucher, a contracted German pilot, who flew many combat missions against rioting tribes. (INA)

providing aircraft and maintenance, Junkers also provided pilots that were hired by the Persian government. Many German and Soviet pilots and mechanics served in the Persian Junkers Company.

Table 3: Soviet pilots, observers and mechanics of JLP

Name	Notes
Tumansky	Flew for JLP April 1924–May 1928
Kudryavstev	Was active in combat until 1927
Vasilchnko	With JLP 1924–1927. Returned to the Soviet Union
Lazovsky	Flew for JLP until 1926. He was also mechanic
Likhanovskye	Flew for JLP 1929–1930. He was also mechanic
Rostov	With JLP until 1925. He was pilot and observer
Ivanoff	With JLP until 1929 as mechanic and observer

German pilot Jüeterbock brought the first Junkers F 13 to Tehran for a demonstration, followed by Messbaucher, Wasserthal, Schaefer and Wagner, who brought rest of the Junkers F 13s to Persia on multiple flights.

Even though these pilots were hired for commercial operations, they were sent into combat when the Persian Civil War erupted and Junkers' services switched to conducting military operations. Since Persian Junkers F 13s served both in civilian and military roles, mechanics often flew as observers or gunners. Most of the German pilots served in combat faithfully with Othello Schaefer even being decorated with the Silver Sepah, the highest Persian military award for bravery, on the Kurdistan front.

Shiraz airport, 1927. (From left to right) 1st Lieutenant Askhar Pishevar, Othello Schaefer, 2nd Lieutenant Bozorg Dayani and Morzik Taumann, in front of three Persian Army Air Corps Junkers F 13s. Their smiling faces are an indication of another successful combat mission against rebellious tribes. (INA)

Famous Swiss aerial photographer and pilot Walter Mittelholzer, together with his mechanic Ernst Bissegger. (Dmitri Kessel)

With the need for military aircraft, the Persian government purchased five of the JLP's F 13s for the Army. One of them was purchased with donations collected from the people of Gilan province for its Northern Brigade that was fighting against the northern rebellions along the Caspian Sea. The aircraft was appropriately named *Gilan*.

In 1924 Junkers started to promote its other aircraft types in Persia. Junkers arranged a demonstration of a Junkers A 20W floatplane. They hired famous Swiss pilot and aerial photographer Walter Mittelholzer and his mechanic Ernst Bissegger. Mittelholzer flew his Junkers A 20W floatplane (c/n 463), registered as CH-130 and named *Ad Astra Co Ltd*, from Zürich to Tehran on 18 December 1924.

Mittelholzer and Bissegger's flight of more than 3,000 kilometres from Switzerland to Persia included a standoff with Turkish authorities during which their aircraft was confiscated.[3] They stayed in Turkey for a month until diplomatic intervention by the Persian government resolved the issue. The airplane was released and the Swiss continued on with their voyage.

However, during the last leg of their flight, the aircraft suffered from a reduction in performance due to the use of poor-quality gasoline purchased in Baghdad. In addition, erroneous maps led them to make a forced landing 40km outside of Tehran, during which the landing gear collapsed. After the aircraft was repaired on spot, it was towed with the help of villagers to a flat area and took off toward Tehran.

During the next few days, the aircraft was flown in an impressive acrobatic demonstration before the authorities in Tehran and Isfahan. The efforts paid off and the aircraft was sold to the Persian government after a new engine was fitted in March. The Swiss pilot and his mechanic stayed in Persia for a month to train two Iranian pilots and a mechanic.

In May, Junkers sent new offers for the A 20 and H 21 and received an order for a second A 20L (c/n 881), which flew from the Junkers Dessau plant via Berlin and Moscow and reached the port of Pahlavi in November. To secure a larger order for the type, Junkers sent four Turkish Air Force A 20s to Tehran on 6 May 1925 to demonstrate combat formation flights. However, this attempt failed and only one Soviet-built A 20, designated R-2 and manufactured by Polikarpov at Junkers' Fili plant, was purchased by donations collected from the people of Mazandaran province. It was therefore named *Mazandaran* and delivered by newly-graduated Persian pilot Lieutenant Issa Khan Tayyar (Shtodakh) to Tehran.

Table 4: Junkers A 20s of the JLP

Type	Registration	c/n	Previous Operator	Delivered	Notes
Junkers A 20W	CH-130	463	Walter Mittelholzer	1924	Initially flew postal service for JLP. Transferred to PAAC as No 21 in 1926
Junkers A 20L	D-361	881	German Junkers Co.	1925	Used as reconnaissance aircraft. DBR, grounded Zanjan, 1929
Polikarpov R-2	R-RFIK	J0890	JLR Moscow	1925	Named *Mazandaran*. Assigned to Northern Brigade. Scrapped in Shiraz as source of parts

Walter Mittelholzer's Junkers A 20W floatplane, registration CH-130 (c/n 463), originally named *Switzerland* (which was later changed to *Ad Astra Co Ltd*). (airwar.ru)

CH-130 being towed by villagers to a flat area to allow it to take-off to Tehran. (Dmitri Kessel)

Walter Mittelholzer at Isfahan, standing on the wing of his A 20L. This aircraft was originally an A 20W floatplane, but was converted to an A 20L landplane in Turkey during its trip to Persia. (Dmitri Kessel)

CH-130 at Isfahan, after flying in from Tehran, for a demonstration flight for the 21st Artillery Brigade commander and personnel. The aim was to impress military authorities to place an order for the type. (Dmitri Kessel)

Delivery ceremony for the second Polikarpov R-2 (c/n 881) at the Junkers Dessau plant, which reached the port of Anzali, Iran, via Berlin and Moscow. VIP guests include the consul, the commerce minister and consulate officials from Persia, as well as Deutsche Bank and Junkers representatives. Note the Persian military roundel already painted on the tail. (Gunther Ott)

1st Lieutenant Issa Khan Tayyar (Shtodakh) sitting on the open cockpit of Polikarpov R-2 *Mazandaran*. (AKTA)

Junkers sent four Turkish Air Force A 35s, in lieu of A 20s, to Tehran for demonstration flights. The people standing in front are (from left to right) Turkish Air Force Mechanic Tudul Kumlik, Turkish envoy Yaral Kumrii and two unidentified British military officers. (Yesil Bursa Tayyaresi)

2

THE ORIGINS OF PERSIAN AIR POWER

Originally intended as a parasol-wing postal aircraft, the A 20 could be easily converted into a light bomber by arming the aircraft with light bombs and a machine gun in the rear cockpit. It could also be used as a reconnaissance or forward air control aircraft. Although there were only three aircraft used in Persia, these A 20s had a remarkable civil and military career.

In the civilian sector, the A 20 was a great airplane to be used for the delivery of mail and small cargo to remote areas in the country – where few airfields were available – due to its capability to land in short distances at unprepared air strips.

Persian Junkers A 20s and F 13s established the first scheduled biweekly air mail service between the capital city and Anzali, Gorgan, Tabriz, Kermanshah, Hamadan, Broujerd, Kazerun, Mashhad, Khoramabad and Khoramshahr.

In addition, a bimonthly service was set up between the capital and all 14 provincial centres. For processing and shipping mail, the Ministry of Post and Telegraph erected service tents adjacent to all serviced airstrips. By the end of 1926, the biweekly postal service was extended to Baghdad, Basra and Kabul.

As a counter to British and Soviet influence, Reza Shah encouraged German commercial enterprises in Iran. By 1926, many large German firms such as AEG, Siemens, Demag, Daimler, Agfa and Bosch had offices, warehouses and processing facilities in various cities throughout Persia. The German *Konsortium für Bauausführungen in Persien* (formed by the three German companies under Philipp Holzmann, Julius Berger and Siemens Baunion) undertook the construction of the Persian Trans Railway network, in collaboration with the Danish firm Kampsax and Czech and Polish engineering companies, which were involved in construction of bridges and tunnels along the railway routes. By order of the Shah, German, Danish, Czech and Polish businessmen – including their families – were allowed to use JLP aircraft at no charge when travelling on official project assignments related to Persian government contracts.

On the contrary, employees of the Anglo-Persian Oil Company (APOC) were banned from using Junkers aircraft, until an official complaint was lodged by the British government to the Persian State Department in 1927. As a result, a Junkers F 13 (D-1126) was leased to the Anglo-Persian Oil Company for the exclusive use of APOC personnel and its affiliated officials, only when flying between Tehran and the oilfields at Ahvaz, Aghajari, Masjid-Suleyman and Haftkel. In addition, a biweekly service using the same aircraft was inaugurated between Tehran and Abadan to transport British Engineers working at the Abadan refinery, which was the largest in the world at the time.

Persian aircraft were not assigned a civilian registration prefix at the time. Therefore, all Persian F 13s used their original German or Soviet registration along with a Persian nickname. These were often the name of a bird, written in Farsi on both sides of the forward fuselage of the aircraft (see Table 1 for details).

JUNKERS IN COMBAT

By early 1926, as commercial routes were spreading throughout Persia, so was tribal unrest and armed riots. The Persian Civil War (1921–1946) was a widespread tribal uprising, which was launched through organised attacks against the federal forces of the central government. These were sponsored by countries that had lost their rights to Persian oil wealth. In order to destabilise the central government, opposition groups were formed in each province and warlords were paid and supported to command these operations.

A rare 1926 photo of a Persian A 20 near Masjid-Soleyman. From left to right: French mechanic Monsieur Banel, Junkers representative Hans Weber, APOC engineer Mehran Bayat, Colonel Ebrahim Arfaa of the 3rd Infantry, German pilot Robert Messbaucher (standing on the port side wing), German engineer Kurt Muller, translator Hakim Mehrmand and customs inspector Ebrahim Nayeb. (Dmitri Kessel)

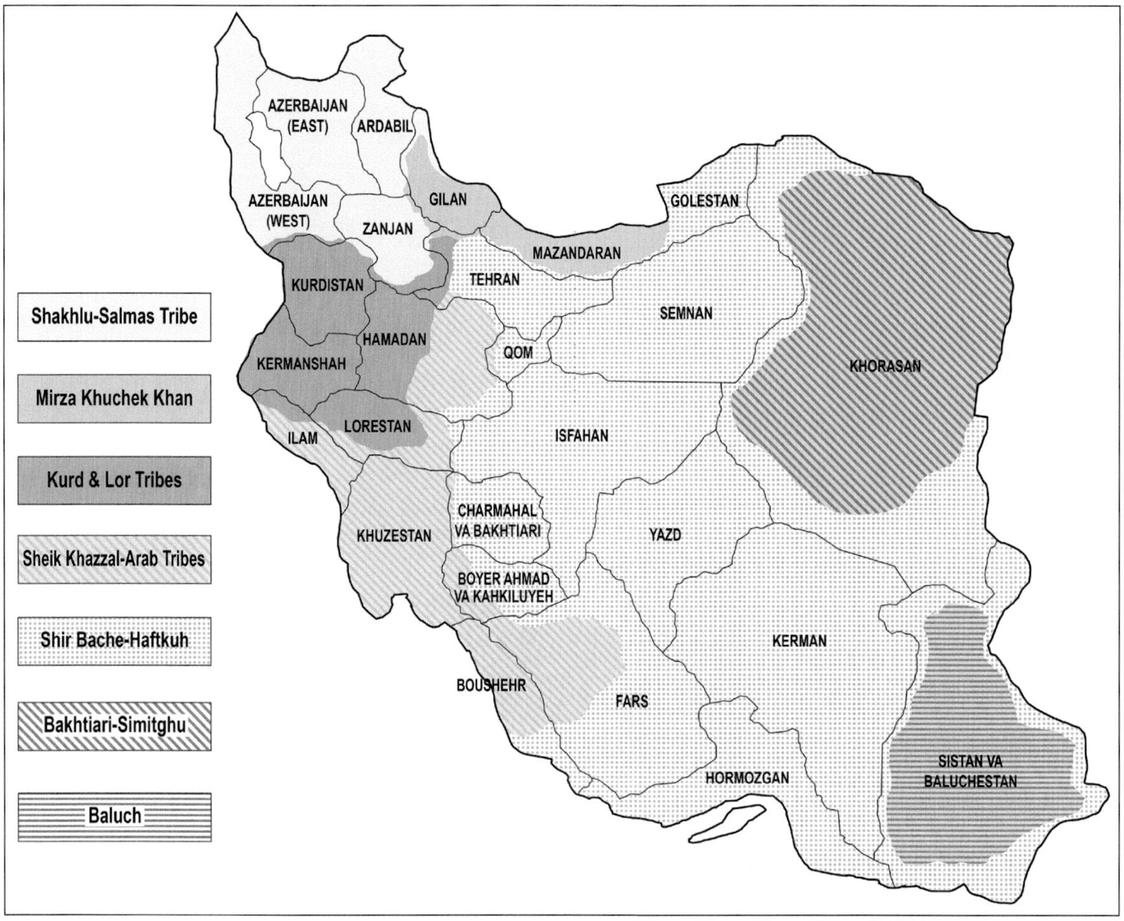

An overview map of the various tribes in Iran that revolted against the Shah during the Persian Civil War (1921–1946). (Leon Manouchehrians)

With the obvious limited power of the ground forces to confront the well-equipped and foreign supported rebellion, Reza Shah was keenly aware of the need for effective air power to counter the tribal offensives in all provinces. In May 1926, he issued a direct order for the formation of the first Air Wing of the Persian Army Air Corps (*Hange-Havai-e-Artesh*).[1]

The newly established air wing consisted of a transport-bomber squadron with five F 13s and a reconnaissance squadron with two A 20s, all based at Ghaleh Morghi airfield.

As F 13s commenced flying operations for the Persian Army Air Corps, they received military roundels and serials, flying various bombing, reconnaissance, and military transport missions to supply food, medicine and ammunition to ground forces as well as transporting injured to army bases for treatment.

For use as a bomber, three F 13s were fitted with locally developed hand rollers in the main cabin to drop 25, 50 and 75lb bombs through an open slot. During 1926 and 1927, over 700 bombs were purchased from the German company Krupp.

Persian pilot 1st Lieutenant Ghahremani takes off in PAAC A 20L serial 21. (Junkers archive)

Persian Junkers F 13 and A 20s played a vital role in military service. During operations against Malakooti rebels in the canyons of the Zagros Mountains, A 20s carried out dive bombing attacks into the very narrow openings of the canyons to take out rebel machine gun positions and destroy their hideouts. While the

Table 5: Insurgent tribes, their leaders and locations

Location	Tribe/Insurgent	Leader	Notes
Gilan/Mazandaran provinces (on the shores of the Caspian Sea)	Jungle Movement	Mirza Kuchik Khan	Soviet-backed and armed
Khuzestan province (Based at Nasseri, present day Khoramshahr)	Bakhtiari	Sheikh Khazzal	Sheikh Khazzal was a British protégé
Lorestan, Kurdistan, Baluchistan, Sistan, Char Mahal Bakhtiari, and Kerman provinces	Lor, Kurd, Baluch, and Bakhtiari	Masoud Barzani	Most populated tribal separatists backed and armed by British
Khorasan province	Ghashghayi	Ilkhani	Soviet-backed Turkish-speaking separatists
Isfahan and Fars provinces	Simitghu Rebels	Esmaeel Simitghu	British-backed and armed
East and West Azerbaijan provinces	Shakhlu-Morovat-Tappeh and Shakhlu-Salmas	Boyanji Dulab	Soviet-backed and armed

results of the bombing attacks are unknown, the use of A 20 parasol aircraft as a dive bomber by itself was significant. Also, in their role as military transport, F 13s moved soldiers to the front, carried out reconnaissance missions and air dropped supplies to ground forces trapped in the snow-packed Sahand Mountains. The fact that these operations were completed without any mishap or accident is a testimony of the skill, bravery and determination of the Persian flyers in defence of their country.

With the ongoing war of attrition between the federal government and the separatist rebels, competition to supply aircraft, ammunition, training and maintenance to the PAAC began between the USSR, Great Britain, Germany and France. In 1929, Junkers representative Kurt Weil met with Reza Shah to submit a proposal to supply a complete air force, including 24 W 33 transports, 12 F 13 bombers, 24 H 21 trainers, 28 A 20 reconnaissance aircraft and 45 K 45 armed fighters.

The K 45 was the militarised version of A 20 with a shorter fuselage and armed with a Kruger-Colt 12.7mm machine gun installed on a ring in the rear cockpit. To promote the sale, a K 45 painted in full Persian markings was sent to Tehran. However, no deal materialised due to intense pressure from Britain and the Soviet Union to purchase their aircraft. In addition, Junkers' failure to establish the promised pilot training and technical schools by 1928 had already damaged the Germans' reputation in Persia.

THE FRENCH CONNECTION

Back in the early 1920s, while Junkers was involved in developing the Persian air transport system, the Soviet Union and Great Britain were trying to get a foothold in Persian military affairs and attempted to increase their influence upon Persian politics in order to receive oil concessions.

A Junkers K 45, an armed variant of the A 20, in full Persian markings at Dessau, Germany before its flight to Persia. (*Flugwelt*)

The Turkish Air Force Breguet 14 B.2 bomber at Tabriz. The aircraft was sent by the French government to promote the type and secure an order by the PAAC. (*L'Avion* archive)

In 1924, Reza Khan, as the commander-in-chief, made a smart political move that was aimed at reducing Anglo-Soviet influence upon Persia. He ordered a delegation, headed by Army chief-of-staff General Amanullah Mirza, to travel to France to select and order French military aircraft for the Persian Army Air Corps.

Taking advantage of the opportunity, the French airplane manufacturer Bleriot further strengthened the French negotiating position, by arranging a demonstration of the combat capabilities of a Turkish Air Force Breguet 14 B.2 bomber variant in Persia on 16 August 1924.

The aircraft remained in Tehran for two weeks during which it was inspected by Reza Khan. In addition, several bombing demonstration flights were arranged for military officials with Persian pilots onboard. The aircraft was well-liked and selected to serve in the PAAC. It is thus no surprise that when General Amanullah Mirza arrived in France, the two-seat Breguet 14 A.2 reconnaissance-bomber was at the top of his shopping list. In less than two weeks of evaluation, four types of French-built aircraft were selected and ordered, which included two Breguet 14 A.2 reconnaissance bombers, two SPAD XIII fighter/trainers,[2] three Potez VIII trainers and a single Breguet 19 A.2 reconnaissance fighter aircraft. Except for the Breguet 19, which remained in France to be flown to Iran by Colonel Nakhjivan (more on that later), all seven aircraft which were taken from the inventory of the French Air Force arrived in containers at the port of Boushehr on 25 and 26 January 1924, along with French pilots René Berhault (*chef de mission*) and Paul Gerard with mechanics Banel and Sigann.

Within two months, all seven aircraft were assembled, flight tested and ready for their ferry flights to Tehran. The three Potez VIII trainers took off in the early morning of 6 March 1924, followed by the two Breguet 14s in the afternoon, while the two SPAD XIIIs left the next day.

On their way to Isfahan during the first leg of the ferry flight, the two Bre. 14s encountered a severe sandstorm some 80 miles south of the city. One of the Bre. 14s flew off course due to high crosswinds and lack of proper navigational equipment and ended up some 90 miles east of its designated route near the city of Naeen. It made an emergency landing on a farm after running out of fuel. It was recovered by local villagers, and the aircraft was carried on a lorry to Isfahan for repairs. The Bre. 14 was repaired by the RAF personnel

Arrival of the first Breguet 14 A.2 at Ghaleh Morghi. Colonel Moghtaderi, the vice commander of PAAC (at right with boots), and State Department French translator Amin-Beyki in white suit. (War Ministry Archive)

The French Potez VIII basic trainer was lightweight and vulnerable to high winds and sandstorms that regularly occur in Persia. Thus, it was unpopular among the pilots. (Aviacion Focal)

stationed there and flew to Tehran on 22 March. The other Breguet 14 was able to reach Tehran without incident.

The other three Potez VIII trainers did not have any better luck. Two of them crash-landed in a sandstorm after their engines quit, while the third made an emergency landing due to an oil leak on a muddy strip near the city of Kashan. All were grounded for weeks and after repairs one was flown by French pilot Paul Gerard to Tehran, while the other two were transported by lorry to the capital.

After all damaged aircraft were repaired, the French biplanes stationed at Ghaleh Morghi airfield formed the first regiment (wing) of the Persian Army Air Corps. In 1926 the wing was moved to Dowshan Tappeh airfield, east of Tehran, where two wooden hangars were built by the French to house their aircraft.

Table 6: List of French-built aircraft in PAAC

Aircraft Type	c/n	Number	Name	Translation
Breguet 19 A.2	n/a	1	*Shahin*	Hawk
Breguet 14 A.2	2424	2	*Parastoo*	Swallow
Breguet 14 A.2	2764	3	*Ghanari*	Canary
SPAD XIII	n/a	J1	*Homa*	Persian Mythical Bird
SPAD XIII	15-295	J2	*Simorgh*	Persian Mythical Bird
Potez VIII	n/a	6	*Morghabi*	Duck
Potez VIII	n/a	7	*Gherghi*	Gargi
Potez VIII	n/a	8	*Gonjeshk*	Sparrow

For more than a year, French pilots and mechanics remained in Tehran and flew the French aircraft for the Persian military. The Shah, however, was not impressed with the quality of these aircraft. Furthermore, he was unhappy that Germany was banned from manufacturing military aircraft as he believed in the superiority of the quality and workmanship of their products and was not interested in any aircraft from other countries.

Although the Potez VIII was a dual-control basic trainer, due to the absence of pilot school in Persia at the time and the lack of interest among young Persians to join the air corps, the Potez VIII fleet was only flown by French instructor pilots stationed at Dowshan Tappeh.

As for the Breguet 14 A.2, it was a modern aircraft for its time. The A.2 variant in French military service was assigned to reconnaissance tasks with a secondary fighter role. This in contrast to the B.2 variant, which was a bomber with a secondary reconnaissance capability. However, despite both Persian Bre. 14s being reconnaissance aircraft of the A.2 variant, bomb racks were added by the manufacturer as an additional feature offered to the Persian government, turning the two Persian Bre. 14A.2s into reconnaissance bombers.

Pulled from French inventory, these aircraft came from different production batches. One of the Bre. 14s was powered by a 300hp (223.8kW) Renault 12 Fe water-cooled, 12-cylinder piston engine, while the other one was equipped with a 320hp (238.6kW) Hispano-Suiza engine. Both aircraft were fitted with flat and focal lens Daguerre 16-8CE and FR cameras installed in the observer cockpit, but devoid of the B-2s' side windows in the rear cabin.

The armament of the Breguet 14 A.2 consisted of a fixed, forward-firing 0.303in (7.7mm) Vickers machine gun on the port side of the fuselage, operated by the pilot from the front cockpit, and a double-yoked pair of 0.303in (7.7mm) Lewis machine guns on a T.O.3 or T.O.4 rotating scarf ring at the observer's station in the rear cockpit. The Michelin bomb rack was mounted under the lower wing, albeit at the cost of reduced speed and range. A total of 32 bombs of

The Breguet 14 A.2 was considered a well-armed reconnaissance airplane. Its Lewis machine gun had a ring around its barrels to prevent shooting towards its tail and stabilisers. The Michelin bomb rack allowed the A.2 reconnaissance variant to carry a total of 560lbs (256kg) of bombs. (Breguet Aircraft)

120mm diameter (17.7lbs/8kg) or an equivalent weight of bombs of other sizes could be carried for a total load of 560lbs/256kg.

The Breguet 14s formed the 1st Reconnaissance-Bomber Unit within the composite squadron based at Ghaleh Morghi. This unit became No.5 Independent Bomber Wing of the 1st Regiment later in 1946 while flying Avro Ansons.

Breguet 14s were extensively used during the Persian Civil War. Imperial Iranian National Archive military documents indicate that the two Bre. 14s were deployed to Yazd, Zahedan, Gorgan, Broujerd, Lorestan and Baluchistan and carried out a remarkable 685 bombing and 106 reconnaissance missions in 1926. Photographs taken by the Bre. 14's Daguerre cameras were processed and printed by the newly established Agfa-Geavert Gmbh laboratory in Tehran in a 9 x 6cm negative format.

During the campaign against the Ilkhani-led Ghashghayi (Qashqai) tribe in the province of Fars, Breguet 14s were used to drop pamphlets urging the separatists to cease fighting. After receiving no positive response, they flew several reconnaissance sorties, photographing the enemy positions, which helped the Army to defeat them by heavy artillery shelling.

Unconfirmed reports suggest that Bre. 14 A.2 serial 2 was sold to Belgium in 1933, while the other, serial 3, is reported to have crashed near the village of Eyvani, in the province of Lorestan, after it was hit by ground fire during a reconnaissance mission in 1931.

PERSIAN SPAD XIIIS

The second French aircraft type to enter Persian service was the SPAD XIII, built by the *Société Pour L'Aviation et ses Dérivés* (SPAD), a subsidiary of Bleriot. Two ex-French Air Force aircraft were refurbished at Dorme, France, after which they were test flown by Sadi-Lecointe (the famous, winning pilot of the Coupe Deutsch air race of 1919). Once tests were complete, both were disassembled and shipped to southern port of Boushehr by the German merchant vessel *Konrad*.

The SPADs arrived a day after the Potez VIII and Breguet 14 aircraft. During their ferry flight to Tehran, one of them made an emergency landing at Kazeroon, while the other aircraft, flown by Bleriot test pilot René Vadim, ran out of fuel due to a faulty gauge and landed near Varamin. It took more than a week until two barrels of fuel arrived on a lorry from Qum. Both aircraft made it to Tehran intact and undamaged, seven days apart.

Upon their arrival they formed the first composite fighter unit in Persian service. The SPAD XIII was a standard model SPAD, and was the most produced single-seat French fighter of the First World War. While classified as a single-seat fighter, it was also used as an advanced combat trainer in Persian service.

The aircraft was fast (with a speed of 130mph) and had a ceiling of 22,456ft, higher than any other aircraft in Persian inventory at the time. Its rigid monocoque fuselage frame was mostly made of duralumin in place of the wood on earlier models, which were entirely covered by fabric. However, its 180hp Hispano-Suiza 8B water-cooled engine was underpowered and did not provide enough torque for its weight, thus the aircraft was not easy to handle, especially during take-off and landing. Due to its comparably small wings, the SPAD XIII had a high stall speed, requiring the pilot to fly the aircraft using tricky manoeuvres in turns and loops during aerial dogfights. After less than a year in service, it was decided to install a more powerful engine on the SPADs to enhance their performance. Two Lorraine Dietrich LO-12Eb engines arrived from France, along with Bleriot chief mechanic Bernard Gaussel, to install the new engines and test fly the aircraft.

In order to encourage the Persian government to place a large order, a Vincent Andre retractable honeycomb radiator was also installed when the aircraft was modified, and the wings were

The first SPAD XIII, serial J1, already in Persian markings after refurbishment at Dorme, France, before its test flight. (*Fondation Francaise de L'aviation*)

With its superb manoeuvring characteristics, the single-seat SPAD XIII was used as an advanced trainer. (Keyhan newspaper -1306)

Bleriot chief mechanic Bernard Gaussel leaning on the SPAD XIII's newly installed engine with a guard in attendance at Ghaleh Morghi hangar. (Aseman-e-Iran magazine)

modified to have single interplane struts and ailerons on both the upper and lower wings.

Additionally, the spatted undercarriage was fully sprung on the main wheel axles. Although these modifications and upgrades enhanced the aircraft performance and handling characteristics, it failed to produce any additional orders. The SPAD XIII was armed with two fixed, forward-firing 7.7mm/0.303 in. Vickers machine guns, that fired through the propeller. During most of its combat missions, hand grenades were also dropped by the pilot.

Persian SPAD XIIIs, like all other aircraft types in service with the PAAC, were used during the civil war against rioting tribes in the southern and central provinces. While the cockpit had armour plating under the pilot's seat for protection against small arms fire, the fuselage, vertical stabiliser, rudder and ailerons were covered with fabric and were often shredded by bullets fired from the ground. In 1929, one of the SPADs (serial J1) stalled during take-off, resulting in a fatal crash, killing its pilot, Lieutenant Jahanshah Mirza. The other aircraft (serial J2) was grounded after it was damaged in a landing mishap in May 1930. It was stored and eventually scrapped in 1932.

The introduction of the fourth type of French aircraft into Persian service is significant. In 1924, the first group of five Iranian cadets was sent to the Istres Flight Academy in France. Among them was a young colonel named Ahmad Nakhjivan. With only 200 hours of flight time under his belt in 1925, newly-graduated Nakhjivan decided to deliver the sole Breguet 19 A.2 fighter-bomber, ordered by the Persian Army Air Corps, to Tehran.

In the early morning of 18 January, he took off from Villa Queily airport near Paris, together with his French mechanic Monsieur Chateaux. He flew eastbound towards Persia, making several refuelling stops en route. These included Venice in Italy, Makdar and Eski-Sehir in Turkey and Halab and Baghdad in Iraq. While landing at Eski-Sehir, his landing gear got stuck in deep mud, which caused the wheel struts and the lower wing to break off.

He remained in Turkey, since the aircraft could not be repaired on the spot. France, however, quickly provided another Breguet 19 A.2 (c/n 292) to Persia at no cost, which made for good public relations. It is worth mentioning that in 1924 the French government had sent a Turkish Air Force Breguet 19 B.2 single-seat bomber to Persia for a demonstration and evaluation, but it failed to generate any large orders and only resulted in the purchase of a single Bre. 19 by the Persian government.

Having received the new aircraft, Colonel Nakhjivan took off again and finally arrived at Tehran's Ghaleh Morghi airfield on 26 January 1925, where Reza Khan was waiting impatiently to

18 January 1925, Villa Queily airport near Paris. Colonel Ahmad Nakhjivan (left) and his mechanic Monsieur Chateaux, standing in front of the sole Persian Breguet 19 A.2, before departing to Persia. (Jaque Lucierre private album)

Colonel Nakhjivan's Bre. 19 being prepared for take-off at Zahedan for a mission against Baluch tribesmen. Sandstorms of the Dashte-Lut (Lut desert) required daily maintenance on its engine filter. (iraviation.com)

Colonel Nakhjivan's Breguet 19 A.2 with damaged landing gear and wings at Eski-Sehir, Turkey. (*Sobhe-Emruz* newspaper)

Colonel Nakhjivan's Br. 19 A.2 under engine maintenance near Paris, a day before his departure for Persia. (Matthieu Comas collection)

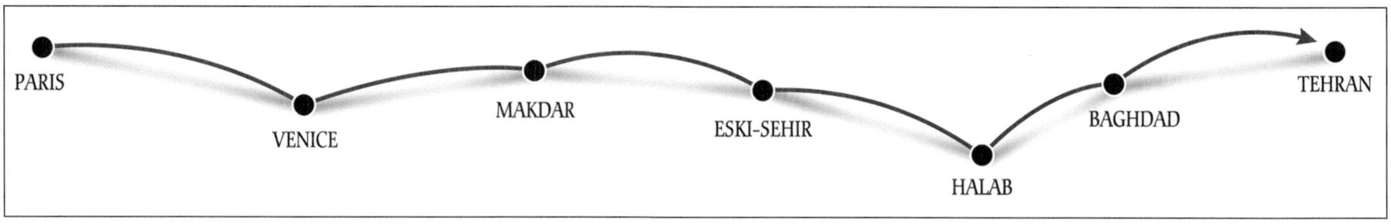

A schematic of Colonel Nakhjivan's Paris-Tehran route and refuelling stops of his ferry flight. (Leon Manouchehrians)

personally greet the newly-graduated pilot. After taxiing in front of the crowd, he got off the plane, kneeled and kissed Reza Khan's hand. The commander-in-chief praised Nakhjivan's attempt to fly the first Paris to Tehran flight in aviation history and became the first Iranian pilot to fly over Tehran in an Iranian-owned aircraft. For his efforts, he was assigned by Reza Khan as the first commander of the Persian Army Air Corps. Colonel Nakhjivan flew over 150 combat missions against Kurdish, Baluch, Turkman, Lor and Ghashghayi rebels in the very same aircraft.

The Breguet 19 A.2 was powered by a 450hp Lorraine Dietrich 2ED inline, water-cooled piston engine and was armed with one fixed forward-firing, synchronised 7.7mm (0.303in) Vickers machine gun, and a pair of double-yoke Lewis machine guns of the same calibre on a T.O.4 scarf ring in the rear cockpit. There was also a provision to attach 15lb bombs and grenades on side racks inside the rear cockpit that would allow these to be dropped by the observer. The aircraft was equipped with a single, floor-mounted, oblique camera of an unknown type which could be operated by the observer. The Breguet 19 served with the 1st Bomber/Reconnaissance Squadron of the 1st Regiment from 1925 to 1929. It remained in service until 1930, when it was stored due to excessive combat use and was finally scrapped in 1931.

A Turkish Breguet 19 B.2 visited Persia in 1924. Sending a demonstration aircraft to promote sales was customary in 1920s and 30s, but in this case it failed to produce a large order. (Turk Havacilik Aylik)

Reza Khan (in the middle with hat) impatiently looking to the sky for the arrival of Nakhjivan's airplane. A large crowd of military personnel and government officials gathered at Ghaleh Morghi airfield. (Iran Military Forum)

3

TRAINING PROGRAMMES

In his role as commander of the Persian armed forces, Reza Shah constantly emphasised the need to replace foreign personnel in the Persian military by Iranians. This required the training of a large number of pilots, mechanics, and observers. With no training facilities available in the country and the failure of Junkers to establish the training school promised for completion by 1928, the Shah issued an order in March 1927 to immediately send Persian cadets to the Soviet Union and France for pilot training.

In April, the first group of seven pilots, that were all hand-picked from the Army's Cossack Cavalry Division, were sent by ship from the port of Anzeli in Iran to Baku in Soviet Azerbaijan. From there they travelled by train via Moscow to the flight academy of Petrograd (current-day St. Petersburg).

The first group of Persian student pilots in front of a Polikarpov-built Avro 504 at the Petrograd Flight Academy in the Russian winter of 1927. Standing from left to right: 1st *Nayeb* (Captain) Sharafedin Ghahremani, 1st Lieutenant Hossein Haghee, 1st *Nayeb* Anvar Aminzadeh, 1st *Nayeb* Taymoor Mobasher and Yavar (Major) Abdollah Najafzadeh. Sitting: 1st *Nayeb* Issa Khan Tayyar, Colonel Vlad Kozminski (Russian instructor) and 2nd *Nayeb* Moheb Aghdani. (AKTA)

POLIKARPOV U-1

In May, another five cadets arrived by train at the Sevastopol Technical Institute in the Crimea on the shores of the Black Sea, while another group of eight was sent to France. The first group of pilots started their flight training at Petrograd with Soviet Air Force Colonel Vladimir Kozminski as their instructor. The Persian cadets regularly flew Soviet Air Force Junkers J 21s, Polikarpov R-1s (license-built DH.9As), and U-1 trainers (U for *uchebnye* or trainer). The latter were licensed copies of the British Avro 504Ks, built by Polikarpov at its plant near Moscow.

Injured pilot Sharafedin Ghahremani stands in front of his U-1 after landing collision with a parked Russian R-1, number 54, at the Petrograd Flight Academy in 1927. This was recorded as the first out-of-country aircraft accident involving a Persian pilot. (*arkhiv voyennoy aviatsii*)

Graduates of Petrograd Flight Academy, Russia

- *Issa Khan Tayyar (1927)*
- *Sharafedin Mirza Ghahremani (1927)*
- *Mehdigholi Mirza Ghahremani (1927)*
- *Ebrahim Bayat Makouee (1927)*
- *Anvar Aminzadeh (observer) (1927)*
- *Fathollah Zand Ansari (1927)*
- *Teymoor Mobasher (1927)*
- *Moheb Aghdani (1928)*
- *Abdollah Najafzadeh (1928)*
- *Mahmood Afshartous (1928)*
- *Farhad Mirza (1928)*
- *Bayandor "Saed Soltan" (1928)*
- *Azizolah Fathee (1928)*
- *Adeli Rafahiat (1929)*
- *Atakhani (1929)*
- *Malek Moezi (1929)*
- *Kambakhsh (1929)*
- *Ahmad Makouee (1930)*
- *Ayram (1930)*
- *Afghami (1930)*

Graduates of Sevastopol Technical Institute, Russia

- *Hossein Haghee (1928)*
- *Masood Diba (1928)*
- *Sepahpoor (1929)*
- *Aziz Fathi (1929)*
- *Abolfatgh Afghami (1930)*

Graduates of Isres Flying School, France

- *Ahmad Nakhjivan (1925)*
- *Ahmad Khosravani (1928)*
- *Mahmood Ghaem-Maghami (1928)*
- *Mahmood Khosravani (obs.) (1928)*
- *Yadolah Azam Zangane (1928)*
- *Khalil Marjan (observer) (1929)*
- *Khanbaba Ala (1930)*
- *Abdolhossein (1930)*

Persian pioneer pilots. (Author's collection)

The Polikarpov U-1 was visually identical to the original Avro 504K. Persian U-1s, duly called *Avrooshka*, had an Imperial crown painted on their fuselage and a Persian tricolour flag on its small tail. (Charles Gray)

The Soviet-built Avro 504, which was duly called *Avrooshka* (little Avro in Russian) by Persian pilots, was one of the best trainers at the time. Just like its original British variant, the U-1 was easy to fly and stable in turns and landing. Liked by Persian cadets, the type was recommended by the students to be purchased by the Persian government. Their suggestions paid off and in 1926, nine U-1s were ordered by Persia after brief negotiations resulted in a barter agreement, where the airplanes were traded in exchange for oil concessions granted to the Soviets in the north-eastern province of Khorasan.

The training of Persian pilots lasted 18 months. At that time, gaining flying wings did not depend on a set number of hours flown on a two-seat trainer, but on merit and the natural flying ability of the cadet. Three of the Moscow-graduated pilots (Issa Khan, Ghahremani, and Zand Ansari) volunteered to deliver three of the *Avrooshkas* to Persia. The other six were crated and shipped to the port of Anzeli, where they could be assembled by Soviet technicians stationed there at the time.

Table 7: List of Polikarpov U-1 aircraft in PAAC

Iranian Serials	c/n	In Service	Previous Operator	Fate
M9	206	1923	Soviet Air Force	Crash-landed, DBR, 1927
M10	211	1923	Soviet Air Force	Sold to Turkey (?), 1929
M11	356	1923	Soviet Air Force	Crashed near Kharkov on delivery
M12	359	1923	New	Destroyed by RAF, August 1941
M13	360	1923	New	Damaged by hangar fire
M14	505	1924	Soviet Air Force	Sold to Palestine (?), 1929 (?)
M15	518	1924	New	unknown
M16	689	1924	Soviet Air Force	Shot down by RAF, August 1941
M17	911	1924	Soviet Air Force	Destroyed on ground by RAF, 1941

On 1 November 1927, the three cadets attempted to take-off from Moscow, but a heavy snowstorm prevented their departure. With most of the cities en route covered with snow, it was decided to send the pilots and crated airplanes by train to the port of Baku, and three days later, the airplanes and pilots arrived there. After assembly, all three aircraft took off towards Tehran on 21 November.

During take-off the engine of Zand Ansari's aircraft failed and the aircraft crashed from low altitude into a muddy field, injuring the pilot. The other two flew on without incident, but during landing at Tehran, Ghahremani's aircraft crashed, due to improperly loaded spare parts in the front cockpit which caused the aircraft to be nose-heavy. The aircraft nosed over into the ground during landing, causing its propeller and wooden skid to break off and the lower wing to shatter when hitting the ground. The Soviets provided replacements for the crashed aircraft and repaired the damaged one. The other six aircraft were flown in by Soviet pilots. These nine U-1s, along with the newly-arrived French trainer biplanes, formed the first training squadron of the Persian Army Air Corps.

By 1928, four of the five cadets sent to France returned to Persia.[1] With unrest and armed riots all over the country, newly-graduated pilots were sent into combat upon their return from training. Actual operational combat training was hands-on for these young pilots who had only a minimal amount of flying time. At times, Persian pilots flew combat missions alongside hired Soviet and German pilots to gain tactical experience until 1928, when most of the hired foreign pilots were dismissed from the service and sent back to their countries of origin. From then on and throughout the 1930s, all combat missions were flown by Persian nationals.

In some instances, Persian *Avrooshkas* were used in combat as bombers, with grenades and light bombs dropped by hand from the observer's rear cockpit. In late 1928, three sets of Michelin bomb racks, purchased as spares for the French-built aircraft, were installed under the U-1s. However, since the 100hp Gnome Monosoupape engine was underpowered, it would not allow more than one 75kg bomb to be carried under each wing of the U-1 when the observer was on board.

One of the U-1s was armed with a Vickers machine gun installed over the wing and was used to strafe rebel columns in Kurdistan and Baluchistan. Persian U-1s received single or double digit serials with a Farsi numeral and the letter 'M', which signified its mission as a training aircraft (*Mashghi*, trainer). While no reliable documentation is in existence, it is likely that the U-1s received the serials M-9 through M-17.

Each aircraft was adorned with the Imperial crown originally painted on the aircraft after delivery. However, this was replaced by a small roundel on both sides of the fuselage, while a crudely painted Persian flag covered its small tail. Large roundels and serials were applied on the top of the high and under the lower wings. Persian U-1s served well into the 1930s and trained 109 pilots in the country.

During the Allied invasion of Iran in August 1941, British forces were surprised to see two airworthy Avro 504Ks, desperately trying to prevent modern RAF fighters from flying into Iranian airspace. One of them was destroyed over Abadan by an RAF Lysander and the other was shot down by an RAF Hawker Hurricane over Ahvaz. The fate of the rest of the U-l fleet is unknown.

Persian pilot Captain Issa Khan Tayyar in front of the first Polikarpov U-1. The skid between the landing gears was to prevent the plane from nosing over during landing. (IIAF archive)

Dropping 25lb bombs by hand was not an easy task for the observer. He had to visually calculate the trajectory of the bomb by taking in consideration of airplane's altitude, speed, angle of dive and wind direction. (WW1 airwarfare)

POLIKARPOV R-3

Concerned by increased British meddling in Persian affairs, the Soviet government offered 40 Polikarpov R-3s to Persia in early 1925, based on the barter agreement established during the purchase of the Polikarpov U-1s.

As a goodwill gesture, four Polikarpov R-3s (license-built Airco – later de Havilland – DH.4s assembled at the Duks (Dux) plant near Moscow) were delivered free of charge. In order to avoid the aircraft delivery being labelled as a bribe, they were marked as a coronation gift for the newly crowned Reza Shah. The aircraft were flown by Soviet pilots from Moscow to Tehran.[2]

The Soviet DH.4 was designated as a bomber and was identical to its original British variant. The four aircraft supplied to Persia were powered by the 260hp M3 engine, itself a copy of the Italian FIAT A9 engine, and were equipped with Soviet-designed dual-cable bomb-release mechanisms. Upon arrival, the aircraft were decorated with the Imperial crown on the fuselage and tricoloured flag on the rudder. These aircraft also received numbers and bird names in Farsi with No.6 called *Gonjeshk* (Bird), No.8 *Kabutar* (pigeon), No.30 *Chelchele* (Swallow) and No.31 *Gherghi* (Gargi). It should be noted that the numbers 6 and 8 and the names *Gherghi* and *Gonjeshk* were previously assigned to Potez VIII trainers.

Despite all efforts by Persia and the Soviet Union, Britain prevented any arms-for-oil deal from being signed. As a result, Soviet plans fell through, and their pilots were ordered to return home. The four gifted R-3s, however, remained in Persia. Britain wasted no time in sending Captain John Colby, a DH.4 instructor pilot, to train Persian pilots to fly the R-3s. By mid-1926, Persian pilots and observers, often used as bombardiers, were in combat with these aircraft and the four R-3s were extensively and effectively used against Kurdish, Baluch and Bakhtiari tribes.

Just like the original DH.4, the Soviet copy was an effective aircraft. It was easy to handle and good in dogfights. While Persian R-3s were not involved in any of these, they demonstrated impressive ground attack capabilities by strafing and bombing enemy columns and installations. Despite its proven effectiveness, the early variant of DH.4 had a major design flaw, which was the separation of its two cockpits that made communication between the pilot and observer difficult. In later production aircraft, as well as the Soviet-assembled

The large, exposed cylinders of the Russian M3 engine considerably obstructed the front view of the pilot. Note the bomb-release cable rack under the fuselage. (Air War Pictorial)

variants with FIAT engines, the higher weight of the engine required the pilot's cockpit to be moved back considerably to maintain the aircraft's centre of gravity and as a result Persian observers did not need to use the 'talking-tube' developed for the type.

Table 8: List of Polikarpov R-3 aircraft in PAAC

Iranian Serials	c/n	In Service	Previous Operator	Fate
6	00-715	1925	Soviet Air Force	Crashed, DBR, Shiraz
8	00-899	1925	Soviet Air Force	Sold to Iraq, 1929
30	02-345	1925	Soviet Air Force	Shot down by ground fire near Lar
31	00-990	1925	Soviet Air Force	Stored 1928 and scrapped in 1931
All four aircraft were assigned to the 1st Regiment bomber wing, stationed at Ghaleh Morghi				

The armament of the R-3 consisted of one fixed forward-firing 7.7mm (0.303 in) Vickers C-8F synchronised machine gun, a pair of double-yoked 7.7mm (0-303) CS-3 Lewis machine guns mounted on type T.O.3 scarf ring in the rear cockpit and a bomb load of 460lbs (209kg).

During combat, one of the R-3s made a crash landing near Nahavand after its engine was hit by ground fire. Pilot *Nayeb* Torab Askani and observer Hakim Mostafavi, both of whom were among the first group of eight pilots trained by British in Persia, were captured and subsequently killed by the rebels.

POLIKARPOV R-1

By late 1925, Polikarpov was putting the finishing touches to the much-improved R-1, the license-built copy of the British de Havilland DH.9A. To restore damaged relations with the Soviet Union, the Persian government sent a letter of interest for the Polikarpov R-1 to Moscow.

In March 1926, a group of three Persians officers (including two pilots) were sent to the Dux plant to evaluate the type. The aircraft was also flown at the Petrograd Flight Academy by both Persian pilots (1st Lieutenant Jahan Malakooti and Captain Torab Shahpasand). Both the delegation sent to the Dux plant and the pilots who made the check flights at the flight academy made favourable reports. This was followed by a short series of negotiations between the Persian Ministry of War and the Soviet government, which resulted an order for 27 Polikarpov R-1 biplanes along with training, spare parts and ammunition.

The Soviet government agreed to train 14 Persian pilots in Moscow and to send an instructor pilot to Tehran to train another 14 in-country. Contrary to many published articles, no R-1s were delivered to Persia before 1926. The first two aircraft (c/n 2501 and 2503) were flown to Tehran by Soviet instructor pilots Vasilchnko and Lazovsky.

Steady delivery of Polikarpov R-1s to the Persian Army Air Corps continued in 1926, with deliveries of two in May, two in August, three in January 1927 and three in June 1927. The aircraft were flown by graduated pilots who returned upon completing their training from the USSR.

By July 1927, the Persian Army Air Corps had 12 R-1s in service. As part of a follow up order in August 1927, nine more R-1s were delivered in crates by rail to Baku. After assembly, the first six took off from Baku on 24 September 1927, but only four reached Tehran as the other two crash-landed due to engine failure en route, eventually reaching Tehran by lorry. Six more R-1s that were ordered arrived by ship at the port of Pahlavi on 22 January 1928. Once assembled, these were flown to Tehran by Persian pilot Issa Khan and Soviet pilots Tumansky, Kudryavstev, Vasilchnko, Likhanovskye, and Lazovsky.

During the delivery of the last batch of the R-1s, four pilots were still undergoing training at the flying section of the Leningrad Aviation Theory School, while six mechanics were undergoing training at the Leningrad Military Technical School.[3]

Despite the test flights of more modern Tupolev R-3 reconnaissance aircraft by Issa Khan in Moscow and overall interest in both this

A Persian Polikarpov R-1, painted in dark grey/brown overall at Dowshan Tappeh airfield. (AKTA)

Delivery of the second batch of R-1s to Tehran. From left to right: Captain Azam Zangane, Captain Khosravani, Lieutenant Haghee, Russian mechanic Lazovsky, Major Ghahremani, Colonel Nakhjivan (with cane), Russian pilot Kudryavstev, Captain Zand Ansari, Captain Mahmoud Khosravani and Lieutenant Issa Khan Shtodakh. (AKTA)

Five Russian pilots (5th, 6th, 7th, 9th and 10th from left), who delivered the second batch of Polikarpov R-1s to Tehran in front of open-door French-built hangars at Ghaleh Morghi. (Lieutenant General Sepahbody, personal album)

aircraft and the Tupolev I-4 fighter, the decision was made to stay with R-1. By March 1928, the 27 R-1s were dispersed within the four regiments (wings) at Tehran, Tabriz, Mashhad and Ahvaz.

Soviet pilot Tumansky returned to the Soviet Union in early 1929, but the other Soviet pilots remained in Persia as instructor pilots. Aside from training, they were hired by the Persian government to fly combat missions in support of the Army against the rebellious tribes. Over 872 hours of combat flying were logged by Persian R-1s during the final stages of war in the Isfahan and Fars Provinces.

By late 1929, tribal attacks by Simitghu, Shakhlu-Salmas and Morovat Tappeh rebels in the Azerbaijan, Kurdistan and Khorasan provinces respectively were largely defeated with the help of the R-1s. Sheikh Khazzal, the leader of Khuzestan separatists, was captured and Mirza Kuchik Khan, the head of 'Jungle movement' in Gilan and Mazandaran provinces, had fled to the Soviet Union.

By contrast, fierce fighting started between the Persian armed forces and armed Bakhtiari, Shir Batche and Haft-Kuh rebels in Lorestan, Fars and Isfahan respectively. In April 1929, a group of six French-trained pilots and four observers was dispatched to Fars and Isfahan with four R-1s, one Junkers F 13, and the sole remaining Breguet Bre. 14 A.2.[4]

The combat was intense as the city of Shiraz was surrounded. The insurgents attacked Shiraz army airfield (today's Shiraz airport), destroying two R-1s and damaging one Junkers F 13. Six Persian pilots flew combat missions with German pilots Schaefer, Wangenheim, and Messbaucher that were still under contract with the PAAC.[5] Foreign mechanics Chateaux from France, Ivanoff from the USSR and Taumann from Germany flew as observers on some of the strike missions.

Persian R-1s were painted dark grey with the Persian flag and the lion and sun emblem on the fuselage. They carried large green-white-red roundels on the top of upper wings and horizontal stabilisers, as well as underside of lower wings. The R-1 was a reconnaissance-bomber (R for *Razviedchik*, Reconnaissance) and served the PAAC with all four regiments. Persian R-1s were powered by Soviet-built M-5 engines, itself a copy of the American Liberty engine but with an improved power-to-weight ratio of 35% (versus 33.5% of the original DH.9A).

The R-1 was armed with a forward-firing 7.7mm (0.303 in) PV-1 (license-built Vickers C-9) machine gun fitted with a Constantinesco C.C. synchronising mechanism and similar calibre DA-2 (license-built Lewis) machine guns on a T.O.2 scarf ring equipped with Hyland Type-B loading handles and Aldis ring-and-bead sights. A Gledhill bomb-release mechanism could deliver two 230lb or four 112lb Krupp-manufactured bombs.

These airplanes formed the backbone of the Persian bomber force and participated on almost every front of the Persian Civil War, including the Fars, Gilan, Khorasan, Khuzestan, Kurdistan, Baluchistan and Lorestan provinces.

Albeit of very poor quality, this photo shows Persian and Russian pilots with two R-1s during their deployment to Kurdistan. (Ganj-e-Jang)

Russian aviator Likhanovskye returns from a bombing mission to Ahvaz. (Mehdi Khosravinejad)

Polikarpov R-1 during a Kurdistan deployment against Shakhlu-Salmas separatists. Two R-1s were lost during the conflict. (aerospacetalk.ir)

Army personnel with their commander (with cape on his shoulder) welcome a PAAC R-1 near Birjand. To the left of the commander is Russian pilot Tumansky (in white overcoat). (AKTA)

Detachments from the 2nd and 4th Regiments were also deployed to Lar, Birjand, Gorgan, and Broujerd. During the conflict, 10 aircraft crashed after being hit by ground fire, and one was set on fire by its own crew after crash landing near Ardakan in order to prevent its machine guns from falling into enemy hands. Another aircraft crashed after hitting a radio broadcast antenna in Boushehr in poor weather. The last R-1 was phased out of Persian Army Air Corps service in 1937.

JUNKERS W 33

With the internal unrest in the country still going on, in 1925, the Persian government decided to purchase more aircraft to expand its air force. As part of the competition between Germany, the USSR and France to sell aircraft to Persia, Junkers once again offered a complete air force, comprising W 33s, two-seat K 45s, and G 24s or G 31s to serve as bombers, fighters and transports respectively.

In order to pitch their sales, Junkers arranged to send a Turkish Air Force, trimotor G 24 to Tehran for a demonstration. The aircraft arrived on 7 December 1925 and Reza Shah personally inspected the G 24 at Ghaleh Morghi, speaking to German pilots Herman Roder and Messbaucher via translator.

Junkers W 33 prototype D-921 was actually a modified F 13, which was used for various trials by Junkers at Dessau. The aircraft was sold to the Persian government at a considerably reduced price. (Junkers)

Junkers' marketing efforts continued with the arrival of a larger Junkers G 31 trimotor from Berlin on 19 September 1927. Due to commonality and prior experience with the F 13, Persia expressed interest in evaluating the W 33 variant for its civilian routes instead. Junkers offered to send the W 33 prototype with registration D-921 (c/n 794) for evaluation. If accepted, the Germans would sell the aircraft at a considerably lower price.

The D-921 itself had been used by Junkers in Germany for various tests before it was refurbished and offered for sale. The W 33 prototype, which was in fact a modified F 13, was eventually purchased by Persia. After modifying the main cabin to add windows, it started a weekly passenger service on the Tehran–Qazvin–Kermanshah–Sanandaj–Hamadan route.

Thanks to the good experiences from service provided by the W 33 prototype, the Persian government ordered six more W 33s between 1924 and 1931, while the Junkers contract was still in force. Two aircraft would be used by the military, while four others were purchased for commercial use.

A Turkish Air Force trimotor G 24 at Tehran on 7 December 1925. Reza Shah (with cane) speaks to German pilot Herman Roder, via translator. (INA)

Junkers W 33 D-1197 *Bolbol* at Hamadan airport after a bombing mission. German technician Adolf Bohme is sitting on the wing. Standing from left to right: German pilot Taumann, Persian Infantry vice commander Major Yavari, 5th Artillery commander Colonel Makoui and German pilot Haan. (Adolf Bohme)

The contract included the cost of modifying the two military W 33s to carry 400lbs of Krupp-made bombs of various weights. Instead of carrying the bombs externally under the wings, they were dropped by roller from a retractable slot in the main cabin floor.

The military W 33s carried a single-barrel machine gun of unknown type and calibre installed in a turret atop the fuselage. They initially received J7 and J8 numbers (J for *Jangi*, Combat) until September 1929, when all W 33 serials were replaced by numbers and bird names.

W 33 D-1590 (msn 2526) was fitted with an Ernemann Heag XV mapping camera under its fuselage, which was used to survey the paths for planned railroad track from Tehran to Hamadan, and from Tehran to Bandare-Gazz on the shores of the Caspian Sea. D-1590 was also involved in transportation of 27 cases of Persian art treasures valued at 1.4 million dollars (29.3 million dollars today) from Tehran to Abadan, from where they were shipped to London for an exhibition at the Royal Academy in September 1930.

By utilising two more W 33s, two new routes were added to Junkers' network in April 1929 and March 1930. The first addition was to the south, connecting Tehran to Isfahan–Shiraz–Boushehr, and the second route was to the west, from Tehran via Qazvin, Kermanshah and Sanandaj to Hamadan, which was later extended

Two peasants from a local village and two ground crew, holding 75lb Krupp bombs, posing in front of a Junkers W 33d. (Lennart Andersson)

Junkers W 33he with serial 11 (formerly J8), written in Farsi numerals on its fuselage, flies a bombing mission. Note the gunner's position on the fuselage roof. (AELR)

Persian army soldiers resting in front of PAAC Junkers W 33 serial J7 near the city of Zabol. The letter J was taken from the Farsi word *jangi* which means combat. The J7 and J8 serials were later changed to No. 35 and No. 11 respectively. (AKTA)

Table 9: List of Junkers W 33s in Persian service

Type	Registration	c/n	Name/Serial	Delivery	Notes
W 33	D-921	794	–	1927	Stored 1933, sold to Zitzmann 1934. Seized by Nazi government in 1939
W 33b	D-1197	2505	*Bolbol* (Nightingale)	1928	Used as bomber-reconnaissance. To Junkers 1930, sold to DVS
W 33b	D-1590	2526	*Tuti* (Parrot)	1927	Used for civil transport and mapping. To Junkers 1928, sold to DVS
W 33c	D-1630	2535	*Oghab* (Eagle)	1931	Used as civil transport. To Junkers 1933, sold to DVS
W 33d	D-1684	2577	*Ghomri* (Bird of Prey)	1929	Used as civil transport. To Junkers 1931, sold to DVS
W 33c3e	?	2757	J7, later changed to No 35,	1929	Rooftop machine gun stand. DBR 1932, Isfahan, scrapped 1934
W 33he	D-OHIN	2770	J8, later changed to No 11	1930	Rooftop machine gun stand. Stored Tehran 1932, back to Junkers in 1944

to Baghdad, Iraq in May 1930. The assignment of bird names to transport aircraft were used for identification of commercial flights.

On 17 December 1930, W 33c3e with military serial 35, delivering a full load of Krupp-made bombs, Soviet-made grenades, ammunitions and fuses, made a crash landing in Shiraz with German pilot Martin Hanichen on the controls. Amazingly, the pilot survived the crash landing without exploding and the plane was repaired by a team of Junkers technicians headed by Adolf Bohme.

The W 33s participated in the highly publicised bombing of Kurdish rebels at Deh-e-Kurd, which resulted in their final defeat in August 1931. Reconnaissance flights were also carried out in Fars and Kerman, during which W 33 J7 was badly damaged by ground fire but was able to land safely near Zarand. In their military transport role, W 33s were used to airdrop food, supplies and ammunition from their side doors, which could be removed for the task.

Due to failure in establishing the promised training and technical schools, the Persian government refused to renew Junkers' contract in 1933. As a result, a decade of superbly safe and effective civilian and military service of the Persian Junkers Company finally came to an end. The expiration of Junkers' contract provided an excellent opportunity for Great Britain to step in and offer the Persian government to establish training and maintenance facilities in-country, which had never been materialised under the German contract.

In June 1929, eight new cadets under command of Colonel Mahmoud Baharmast were sent to France. However, training Persian pilots in small quantities in foreign countries was financially uneconomical and unacceptable for Iranian national prestige.

Britain offered to supply training aircraft and help expand the Persian air force training facilities. With the failed Junkers contract and the continued Soviet backing of the Jungle Movement separatist rebels in Gilan and Mazandaran provinces, the British plan was accepted by the Persian government. As a result, the first group of British military advisors arrived in Persia in May 1933.

With British support a number of facilities were established as detailed below.

Perhaps the only photo in existence of this aircraft, under the watchful eyes of guards, Junkers W 33d D-1590 *Tuti* is being loaded with Persian artifacts for transfer to Abadan to be shipped to London for an exhibition at the Royal Academy in September 1930. (AKTA)

A ground marshaller uses a stick to give take-off clearance to Junkers W 33d D-1684 with *Ghomri* written in large letters on both sides of the fuselage. (Volker Koos)

Junkers W 33c3e, with serial 35 written under its wing, survived the crash landing at Shiraz while carrying a full load of bombs, ammunition and fuses. It was repaired by Junkers technicians and returned to service. (Lennart Andersson)

The Persian Army Air Corp Junkers W 33b D-1197 used as a bomber-reconnaissance aircraft, photographed at Isfahan airport. (Junkers)

Flying School

Established in September 1933 at Ghaleh Morghi airfield. The facility was later relocated to Dowshan Tappeh airfield (some 4km east of Tehran), which was also constructed by Britain. It was later renamed Aerial Military Institute. The remaining three U-1s were used for basic training pending the order of a new trainer aircraft.

The first 23 pilots that graduated from the flying school included Lieutenant Ali-Asghar Malek, who became the first Persian pilot graduated in Persia, with the second group consisting of 18 pilots, including Lieutenant Saeed Ezazi (later General and deputy commander of the IIAF), Hassan Toofanian (later General and head of defence procurements), and Ali Mohammad Khademi (later Lieutenant General and CEO of Iran Air).

Until its closing following the Allied invasion in August 1941, the pilot training school completed eight training classes and a total of 213 pilots graduated.

Technical Training School

Established in February 1934, at Ghaleh Morghi. During its first class, 23 technicians graduated from the 10-month course and were assigned to combat units for base maintenance. Later, the maintenance school was moved to Dowshan Tappeh and was renamed the Military Technical Institute.

In 1936, a new branch called tooling and manufacturing, was established within the technical school to train aircraft parts production technicians for the planned Shahbaz State Aircraft Factory (more on that later).

Eight classes were completed by the technical school until its closing in August 1941. Directors of the school for the eight classes were Captain Mahmoud Khosravani, Major Khalil Marjan, Major Amin Zadeh and Colonel Placid.

Advanced Pilot Training School

Established at Mehrabad airfield in March 1935. When in 1947 Mehrabad became the main operational base with no fewer than six fighter, bomber and reconnaissance squadrons, the training school facilities (along with its Hawker Hinds and de Havilland DH.82 Tiger Moths training aircraft) were transferred to Dowshan Tappeh airbase.

The four British instructor pilots of the advanced flying school trained no fewer than 314 pilots in eight training classes. The graduating pilots received their flying wings after completion of advanced aerial combat tactics, bombing and reconnaissance courses that followed standard RAF syllabuses.

Air Observation College

Established in June 1933, at Dowshan Tappeh. In the first term, 18 observers completed their one-year course, 10 of whom advanced to the flying school for pilot training. From 1939, Air Observation became one of the courses of the Army Officers' Academy.

Weapon Specialist College

Established in March 1934 at Dowshan Tappeh.

Instructor Pilot School

Established in May 1935 at Dowshan Tappeh. The first term provided nine instructor pilots who graduated in 1936. The school was later moved to Mehrabad, but returned to Dowshan Tappeh in 1947.

POLIKARPOV R-5 VS POTEZ 25

On 4 September 1930, three Soviet Polikarpov R-5 biplanes, with serial numbers USSR-351, -352, and -353, landed in Persia. This flight, under the direction of Feliks Inganius and Ivan Spirin, three Soviet pilots (Fedor Shirok, Yakov Shestel, Aleksandr Mazinov) and journalist Mikhail Koltsov, was part of the 'Great Eastern Tour', organised by Polikarpov for propaganda purposes. The tour started in Moscow and flew through the cities of Kyiv, Sebastopol, Ankara, Baku, Tabriz, Tehran, Termez, Kabul, Tashkent and Orenburg, after which it returned to Moscow on 30 September 1930.

Dressed in typical flying gear of the 1930s, 48 pilots are gathered at Dowshan Tappeh airfield during graduation ceremony on 14 July 1938 after completion of their basic training on Tiger Moths. (iiaf.net)

Russian Polikarpov R-5, USSR-353, at Baku during refuelling. The three R-5s of the Great Eastern Tour flew through Tabriz, Tehran, Termez, Kabul, Tashkent and Orenburg, after which they returned to Moscow on 30 September 1930. This propaganda flight secured an order for 10 Polikarpov R-5s for the PAAC. (airwar.ru)

This bold 26-day tour covered 10,500km, logging 62 hours and 45 minutes of flying time with an average speed of 170.5km an hour. Flying in very harsh conditions through several countries, a great amount of logistical planning was needed to complete the long journey. Besides being a matter of prestige for the Soviet Union, the flight was primarily intended to be a sales campaign that ultimately led to the sale of R-5 aircraft to the three countries it flew through.

The USSR did not hesitate to mention to their hosts that these were the most modern aircraft available. Turkey did not show interest in purchasing the Soviet biplane, albeit in 1936 they used the type in very small numbers for communication purposes. The USSR initially failed in Afghanistan as well, because of a cholera epidemic and civil war going on at the time. However, six years later the Soviets set up a civil aviation route between Kabul, Kandahar and Tashkent using a small number of P-5s (a modified version of R-5) as transport aircraft.

On 18 October 1930, the Soviets sent a proposal for the sale of 30 Polikarpov R-5 biplanes to Persia. The Soviet proposal came exactly at a time when Persia, following its 1929 negotiations with the French Potez and Lorraine Company, was about to place an order for 10 of the new Potez 25 aircraft, plus an option for an additional 30. The Soviet campaign and the Great Eastern Tour, however, proved successful in Persia. Polikarpov succeeded in selling 10 R-5s to Persia, despite strong British efforts to block the sale.

Several factors played a role in ordering the first military aircraft from the USSR. First, the Soviet offer accepted trading agricultural materials in exchange for the aircraft. This was perhaps the first agricultural barter contract recorded in Persian history. Second, the purchase of a new aircraft was in line with Reza Shah's modernisation programme to expand the air force. Third, this sale fitted the Persian government policy at the time to maintain a commercial and political balance between Eastern and Western powers.

While the French Potez 25 was clearly a much more modern aircraft and superior to the R-5, the selection of the Soviet plane could only be explained as to secure an alternative source of military supply in case the European countries cut their ties with Persia over oil disagreements.

The decision was a major loss for the French government, since they assumed the sale of the Potez 25, albeit in small quantities, would make France the sole provider of the future aircraft to Persia. However, the French put pressure on the Shah to overturn the Soviet order. Pressure increased to the point that in October 1930, Reza Shah agreed to hold a multi-level competition between three R-5s and a single Potez 25 to finalise the fate of the previously negotiated deal with the French. The Soviets wanted to win this competition because of their unfavourable relation with France and to gain influence in Persia by selling the 30 additional R-5s as proposed in the contract.

On 28 October 1930, three R-5 biplanes arrived at Ghaleh Morghi airfield after a long flight from Moscow. Because of the high mountain ranges located throughout Iran, a 6,000 metre minimum altitude was imposed by the Persian government. The R-5s reached an altitude of 6,700 metres, surpassing the minimum requirement.

In all fairness, it has to be noted that the R-5s used in this competition were powered by uprated 685hp M-17F engines instead of their standard 500hp M17B engines. In addition, the Soviet aircraft were stripped of all photographic equipment, radios, bomb racks and cables, which they would normally have carried as part of their standard mission payloads. As a result, their range was extended from 900km to 1,400km, the entire distance from Tehran to Shiraz. Their airspeed with a full payload was also increased from 150kph to 210kph.

The French rightfully protested, and the Persians declared the competition a tie. Nevertheless, the Shah ordered a new competition in 1931. When only Polikarpov responded to the invitation, the French did not participate in protest at the decision of the previous competition. As a result the Potez 25 proposal was officially cancelled.

On 28 May 1933, Persian pilot Lieutenant Ebrahim Makouee delivered the first R-5 from Moscow to Tehran via Kharkov and Grozny. In an attempt to complete the flight in one day, he was forced to fly the last leg from Baku to Tehran at night. As a result, Makouee recorded the first night flight in Persian aviation history. The other nine aircraft were shipped in crates to the port of Anzeli, where they were assembled by Soviet technicians and flown to Tehran by Persian pilots with refuelling stops in Rasht and Qazvin. Persian R-5s were assigned serials 30 to 39.

The negotiated contract for 30 additional R-5s was cancelled by the Persian government after its intelligence services discovered that a Soviet spy network had decoded telegram messages between the Persian and French governments before the first competition. This had given the Soviets a considerable advantage over the French entry.

As punishment for cancelling the negotiated agreement, the 10 Polikarpov R-5s were delivered with limited spare parts, which included only two engines and 12 tires. Later in January 1939, two sets of skis were delivered for use by the 2nd and 3rd Regiments at Tabriz and Mashhad, during the winter season at the northern provinces of Azerbaijan and Khorasan respectively.

The R-5s participated in the suppression of the 1935–36 tribal uprising in Fars, Isfahan, and Kurdistan, performing reconnaissance and bombing missions in Gonbad-e-Ghabus, Khoramabad, Gonabad, Ilam and Kermanshah. During bombing missions in 1935 against Baluch and Ghashghayi tribes in Fars province, Soviet-supplied DFV-01 bombs were used by the R-5s. Each aircraft could carry a maximum of 550lbs of bombs on four pylons under each wing. Only four of the Iranian R-5s were armed with fixed forward-firing PV-1 machine guns operated by the pilot and a flexible DA machine gun in the rear cockpit.

Upon their delivery, after the Iranians complained about the absence of armament on the rest of the fleet, the Soviets claimed that the factory was closed due to technical and financial difficulties and that the weapons would be delivered and installed at a later date. This promise, however, was never realised and therefore only four armed R-5s were used for close air support, while the rest were assigned to reconnaissance missions using their Soviet 6 x 6 large format Komsomolets-ARFO-Artel Foto-Trud cameras.

The only known photograph of a Persian ski-equipped Polikarpov R-5, serial 36, taken on a snowy winter day at Ghaleh Morghi. Only two sets of skies were delivered to PAAC for use in the northern provinces of Azerbaijan and Khorasan. (AKTA)

PAAC Polikarpov R-5, serial 33, getting ready to take-off for a combat mission from a desert strip near Yazd in central Iran. The Iranian hot-and-high environment was not ideal for a Russian aircraft designed to operate in cold weather. (Lennart Andersson)

Polikarpov R-5, serial 30, photographed during a formation flight consisting of three aircraft, one unarmed equipped with a camera and the other two armed with machine guns as escorts. (AELR)

Polikarpov R-5, serial 32, seen in the open desert near Kashan. The four underwing pylons, used to carry bombs and fire canisters (not delivered to PAAC), are clearly visible. (Farokh Foundation)

By 1939 the R-5 fleet was reduced to four flyable aircraft with only one fully armed, the result of two crashes and the grounding of four others due to refusal of the USSR to supply additional parts. Since the R-5 was primarily designed for USSR's cold weather, its flying characteristics were considerably diminished due to the hot-and-high conditions present in Persia. The poor performance of R-5s, even with improved M-17F engines, in comparison to the British Hawker aircraft, relegated their role in the IIAF from reconnaissance-bomber to advanced trainer. The unsatisfactory service of R-5s, coupled with continuous aggression by the USSR in the northern provinces of Gilan, Mazandaran, Khorasan and Azerbaijan, permanently ended the use of Soviet equipment in the Iranian air force.

THE TIGER MOTH

In May 1932, Great Britain sent an Avro 626 trainer, registration G-ABRK, to Tehran for a demonstration flight, but the type was not approved for purchase. Captain Alis Nordquist, along with Colonel Issa Khan and Major Arfaa, were sent to England to choose a trainer aircraft, since they were in charge of all military purchases from Europe. After evaluating several different types of training aircraft, the de Havilland DH.82 Tiger Moth was selected. An order for an initial batch of 20 120hp Gipsy-III powered aircraft followed soon.

In December 1932, the new trainers arrived in crates at the port of Khoramshahr. de Havilland sent its chief pilot Hugh Buckingham and chief mechanic Brett Johnson to supervise the assembly and testing of the aircraft, expecting that this would smoothen the delivery and pilot transition to the new type, leading to further orders from Persia.

The Tiger Moths were assembled and flown to Tehran via Ahvaz in three groups between 12 December 1932 and 23 January 1933. However, one aircraft piloted by Persian pilot Fatollah Zand Ansari crashed during delivery. Sadly, this marked the first non-combat Persian pilot fatality in the country.

The second batch of nine (and not 10 as mentioned in many records) aircraft was powered by uprated 130hp Gipsy Major engines. These aircraft were designated DH.82A and were ordered in 1933. By 1940, a total of 99 Tiger Moth planes, including 20 DH.82s and 79 DH.82As, had been delivered to Persia in 11 batches. In 1939 and 1940, 10 more DH.82As were assembled by the Shahbaz State Aircraft Factory at Dowshan Tappeh, bringing the Tiger Moth fleet to a total of 109 aircraft. Aside from the 51 aircraft assigned to the Mehrabad advanced training school, the rest of the fleet was dispersed within the four regiments.

Eight of the principal officers of the Persian air force standing in front of the first de Havilland Tiger Moth of a batch of 20. Fourth from the left is General Ahmad Nakhjivan, commander of the air force. On his right is Captain Azami, commander of the flying school at Tehran. The photograph was taken at Ahvaz by Mr. Buckingham, who was responsible for the handover of Tiger Moths in Persia. (Buckingham collection)

Photographed at Dowshan Tappeh, DH.82A Tiger Moth, serial 156, (c/n 3306) from the fourth batch of 20 was delivered in 1935. It was powered by a Gipsy Major engine. (IIAF)

Table 10: List of DH.82 Tiger Moths delivered to Iran

Batch	c/n	Qty	IIAF Serials	Engine	Delivery	Manufacturer
1	3117–3136	20	101–120	Gipsy-III	1932	de Havilland
2	3200–3208	9	121–129	Gipsy Major	1933	de Havilland
3	3228–3237	10	130–139	Gipsy Major	1934	de Havilland
4	3290–3309	20	140–159	Gipsy Major	1935	de Havilland
5	3464–3473	10	160–169	Gipsy Major	1935	de Havilland
6	3930–3934	5	170–175	Gipsy Major	1938	de Havilland
7	82005–82009	5	176–180	Gipsy Major	1938	de Havilland
8	82047–82051	5	181–185	Gipsy Major	1938	de Havilland
9	82092–82096	5	186–190	Gipsy Major	1938	de Havilland
10	83352/53/55	3	191–193	Gipsy Major	1939	de Havilland
11	83357–83363	7	194–200	Gipsy Major	1940	de Havilland
12	83774–83783	10	201–210	Gipsy Major	1939/1940	Shahbaz

The ease of flying and maintenance of the Tiger Moth made it the favourite trainer aircraft among Persian pilots and mechanics alike. Six Tiger Moths had their back seats covered by a black tarpaulin for instrument and night flight training known as 'blind flying' at the time.

The Tiger Moth was a dual-control aircraft and could be flown from either cockpit. Three sets of floats and two sets of skis were also ordered with the second batch of aircraft, although it is not known if any of floats or skis were ever delivered or used.

With the civil war still going on, the versatility of Tiger Moth allowed it to be utilised in additional roles such as light bombing, army cooperation, observation, and ambulance. For combat missions, 38 Tigers were fitted with cable-operated bomb-release mechanisms to carry 21 and 32lb bombs. Due to a shortage of observers in the early 1930s, the Persian air arm used aircraft mechanics to perform air observation and photography duties, as well as shooting handheld rifles and throwing grenades from the back seat.

Lineup of Tiger Moths at Dowshan Tappeh, with 130 in the foreground and 166 behind it. The 109-strong Persian Tiger Moth fleet was effectively utilised for three daily training syllabuses. A group was set for basic training with three one-hour flights at sunrise, a mid-day group performed navigation training with two 1.5 hour flights, and a group flew two one-hour flights at sunset for advanced training. (History of IIAF)

One of six Tiger Moths fitted with covered cockpits for 'blind flying' training. The instructor in the front cockpit had to communicate with the trainee through a talking-tube. (IIAF)

A formation of four Tiger Moths on a close air support mission over the city of Bam in the Central Desert. Their armament consisted of handheld rifles and grenades dropped by hand from the back seat. For such missions, the pilot flew the plane from the front seat. (AELR)

SWEDISH AND BELGIAN ADVISORS

In January 1932, Swedish Captain Alis Nordquist was hired as chief advisor to the Persian air arm to set up a modern air force administration and headquarters' staff office. Within three months, he established the staff headquarters and became the Persian air arm's first chief-of-staff.

In December 1932, another Swedish advisor, Lieutenant Erik Ekman, was hired as an instructor for a year to speed up the training programmes and to teach advanced tactics used by European air arms. He arrived in Tehran in January 1933. By January 1934, four more Swedish instructor pilots were hired by the PAAC. These were Fredrik Johansson, Stig Sundgren, Gunnar Cornelius and Floryik Schollin.

In April 1934, Captain Nordquist left Iran and was replaced by a Belgian officer in November. Major Victor Bevir, who was promoted to the rank of colonel by a direct order of Reza Shah, became the Persian Army Air Corps' second chief-of-staff.

In 1934, the training programme was expanded with the arrival of four Belgian air officers (Guillaume, Geris, Van Damme and Pito) along with six other high-ranking Belgian pilots (among them Boshen, Formal and Schwartz). The first group of four arrived in November and the other six in January 1935.

However, despite improved training and safety procedures, Tiger Moth accidents and crashes were numerous. As mentioned before, the first crash occurred during the delivery flight of the first batch from Ahvaz to Tehran. On 8 March 1933, just a mile south of Ghaleh Morghi airfield, a formation of three Tiger Moths returning from solo training attempted to turn towards the airfield in close formation. During the turn, the right wing of the left wingman flown by Lieutenant Fathi collided with the left wing of Lieutenant Kayhan Ghaem-Maghami, who was flying as the right wingman. The wings were entangled for a few seconds and after they separated, both aircraft entered an uncontrollable spin. Lieutenant Ghaem-Maghami's aircraft crashed at a steep angle, killing the pilot instantly, but Lieutenant Fathi was able to level the aircraft, hitting the ground on its belly and surviving the crash with major injuries to his spine. This incident was recorded as the first mid-air collision in Persia.

According to old maintenance records, at least 26 Tiger Moths were marked as crashed or damaged beyond repair in Persian service. There were several contributing factors. First, the aircraft's light weight made it prone to accidents during crosswind landings and sandstorms. Second, the lack of proper training in manoeuvres could easily result in putting the biplane in an irrecoverable spin with often fatal results. The third reason was that most landing strips in Persia were unpaved and rain would turn these into muddy fields in a very short time. This could cause the landing gear to get stuck in the mud during landings, resulting in the aircraft to nose over and possibly damage the propeller, engine and wings and injure the pilot.

The de Havilland DH.82 and 82A Tiger Moth replaced all the older trainers in Persian service. The type rendered magnificent service for over two decades and trained over 300 Iranian pilots throughout its service in the PAAC and IIAF, until they were replaced by North American T-6 Texans in the early 1950s. Almost every veteran pilot from Iran, even the ones who went on to fly the F-4 Phantom II, F-5 Freedom Fighter and Tiger II and even the F-14 Tomcat, fondly remember their basic training on the Tiger Moth.

By 1953, only a handful of Tiger Moths were still in Iranian service. Iranian records also indicate that in 1939–40, six air force DH.82s, along with military instructor pilots, were transferred to the Imperial Iranian Aeroclub (*Bashgahe-Havapeymayei-e-Shahanshahi*) for civil pilot training. These aircraft remained in civilian service until the delivery of 25 Rearwin Cloudsters to the club in 1941.

Belgian Major Victor Bevir was promoted to the rank of colonel by direct order of Reza Shah to become the second PAAC chief-of-staff. (Sobhe-Emruz)

Above: Lieutenant Ghaem-Maghami with Tiger Moth 108 at Dowshan Tappeh, four months before he died in a crash. (iiaf.net)

Right: Four Tiger Moths, 105 in the foreground, at Dowshan Tappeh, ready for training flights. The snow-packed Alborz mountain range north of Tehran is visible in the distance. (Fredrik Lambert-Moller)

4

THE GOLDEN 1930s

During the 1930s, British dominance of Persian military affairs was at its peak. This was the direct result of the successful introduction of the Tiger Moth for training large numbers of Persian pilots and British government assistance in establishing flying and maintenance schools and the construction of new airfields in Persia. Thus, when the Persian air force started to search for more modern aircraft to expand its combat capabilities, it was not to anyone's surprise that the replacements would be of British origin.

In the period from 1933 to 1938, three types of British-built fighters, bombers and operational trainers entered Persian service. These were the Fury, Audax and Hind biplanes, all built by the Hawker Aircraft Company at Kingston and Brooklands in the United Kingdom.

It is worth mentioning at this point, that Reza Shah made a visit to Turkey in 1934. This was his only visit to a foreign country, where he witnessed Turkish economic progress, industrial developments, as well as its military installations and equipment. Impressed with the number of personnel, aircraft and airfields of the Turkish Air Force, he aimed to build a similarly effective and sizeable air force for which he was ready to accept any assistance from any country. Thus, the Shah's visit played a large role in accepting British offers to rebuild his air force with British aircraft and technical assistance.

HAWKER FURY

Developed from the Hawker F.20/27 prototype, the Fury single-seat interceptor fighter was the first RAF aircraft capable of flying faster than 200mph to enter squadron service. With its sensitive controls, high rate of climb and outstanding manoeuvrability it was considered one of the finest biplane fighters of its day. Sixteen Hawker Fury Mk.Is were ordered by the Persian government in January 1933 under contract No.100118/33 to equip one squadron of the PAAC. However, the order was later reduced to 12 Furies as four additional Audaxes were ordered in their place.

The Persian government made an extensive agreement with the Pratt & Whitney Company for the purchase and servicing of the big S2B1-G Hornet radial engines that were to equip the Persian Furies. The 750hp engines were specified to be equipped with metal three-bladed Hamilton Standard Hydromatic propellers, despite the fact that the standard two-bladed, large coarse-pitch Watts wooden propeller was tested for comparative standards during initial evaluation trials at Brooklands.

Even when equipped with the Watts propeller, nose heaviness resulted in taxiing difficulties. Following an accident in Martlesham, United Kingdom, a tail ballast was installed to slightly move the centre of gravity towards the tail to improve balance. Deliveries of the first batch of six Hornet-powered Furies started in July 1933. Upon arrival in Persia, they received serials 201 to 206. After just a few days of service in Persia, a problem with overheating occurred due to the Hornet's shutters providing insufficient air for engine cooling. The hot-and-high conditions of Persian airfields also contributed to the problem. As a result, the second batch of six Furies that was ready for delivery had their engines changed to the 550hp Bristol Mercury VISP ('P' for Persia).

A Hawker Fury (serial 203) was used to test the aircraft with the Mercury engine in September 1934. After tests were successful, the second batch of Furies (with serials 207 to 212) from the first order

One of the six Hawker Fury Mk.Is of the first batch, serial 203, with the big and heavy Pratt & Whitney S2B1-G Hornet radial engine and three-blade Hamilton metal propeller, during a static test at Brooklands, United Kingdom. (Aeroplane)

Hawker Fury Mk.I, serial 203, during its first test flight with the Hornet engine at Kingston, UK. (Profile series)

Comparing two engines. Top: Fury serial 204 with the Pratt & Whitney S2B1-G Hornet engine equipped with a three-blade Hamilton metal propeller. Bottom: Fury serial 203, re-engined with the Bristol Mercury VISP fitted with a 2-blade wooden Watts propeller. (Hawker archive)

had their engines converted and arrived in Persia during the months of November and December of 1934. The surplus Pratt & Whitney Hornet engines were used to equip the first batch of Persian Audaxes.

With the need for more Furies in Persia, a provisional order for 30 additional aircraft was placed with Hawker Aircraft Ltd. When finalised, the second order under contract No. 366843/34 covered only 12 Fury Mk.IIs, which were powered by 605hp Bristol Mercury VISP-II engines. Deliveries commenced in January 1935. Upon arrival delivery, these aircraft were assigned serials 213 to 224.

From the last batch of 12, this Hawker Fury Mk.II, serial 216, powered by a Bristol Mercury VISP-II engine, is photographed at Tabriz during operations against Morovat Tappeh insurgents. (AirFan)

Hawker Fury Mk.I, serial 203, was also used for testing the British Bristol Mercury engine with a two-blade Watts propeller. (Aircraft Illustrated)

Hawker Fury Mk.I, serial 208, from the second batch of the first order which was already fitted with Bristol Mercury engines, during a test flight at Brooklands, UK. (Aeroplane)

Table 11: List of Hawker Furies delivered to Iran

Type	Engine	Qty	IIAF Serials	Manufacturer	Delivery
Hornet Fury	PW S2B1-G Hornet	6	201–206	Hawker	July 1933
Mercury Fury	Bristol Mercury VISP	6	207–212	Hawker	November–December 1934
Fury Mk.II	Bristol Mercury VISP-II	12	213–224	Hawker	January 1935

Persian Furies served with the 1st Regiment at Ghaleh Morghi, which was also the centre for training new pilots with around 40 Tiger Moths based there as part of the regiment. The new Persian Furies were undoubtedly attractive little fighters and upon delivery to the Persian air force embarked on a long and interesting career.

During the Kurdistan conflict, a large detachment of Hawker Furies from all four regiments was deployed to Maku and Piranshahr in support of the Army. They flew close air support missions by strafing Kurd insurgent's columns along the canyons of the Sahand and Sabalan Mountains. For deployment to combat in remote areas, Persian Furies carried desert stores under the wing.

The flightline of Hawker Fury Mk.Is as part of the training squadron of the 1st Regiment at Ghaleh Morghi. The first aircraft is 205. (History of IIAF)

With the Zagros Mountains as backdrop, 11 Hawker Furies are seen on the flightline during their deployment to Kermanshah to counter Bakhtiari revolts. (*Przegląd Lotniczy-Aviation Revue*)

Hawker-supplied desert stores were carried under the wing by Furies and Audaxes when these were deployed to remote areas. They could carry essential items such as drinking water, medical supplies, food container, pistol ammunition, and engine oil. (F.K. Mason collection)

Deployment of Hawker Furies to northeast province of Khorasan, near the city of Ghuchan (Quchan), during operations against Ghashghayi-Ilkhani tribes in 1936. The six pilots on the left and four mechanics on the right are all wearing winter overcoats. (History of IIAF)

Colonel Majid Moradi and 1st Lieutenant Fereydon Biniaz in front of their Fury 216. Their airplane was hit and crash-landed. They were captured and killed by Kurdish insurgents. (AELR)

During the operations against Baluch tribes in summer of 1935, 16 pilots were dispatched to Sistan and Baluchistan province, of which three were killed and four aircraft were destroyed. Among them were two instructor pilots, Colonel Majid Moradi and 1st Lieutenant Fereydon Biniaz, who made a crash landing after their Fury was hit by ground fire. They were captured and killed by the rebels.

In 1936, Persian Hawker Furies visited Syria, Palestine, Egypt and Libya as part of an Islamic Countries Friendship Tour. The Iranian Keyhan newspaper reported on 17 June 1936 that the Iranian Hawker Furies were flown for type trials by *Regia Aeronautica* (Italian Air Force) pilots stationed in Libya.

In August 1941, during the Allied invasion of Iran, two Furies engaged in dogfights with No. 261 Squadron RAF Gloster Gladiators and Hurricanes over Ghasre-Shirin. Both Furies were shot down. Another four attempted to attack Nos. 11 and 84 Squadron Bristol Blenheim Mk.IVs over Abadan and Ahvaz respectively, but were also shot down. Another Fury was destroyed by a strafing Hawker Hurricane, while taxiing for take-off at Aghajari airfield.

As late as 1942, one squadron of about 10 Fury Mk.IIs was based at Mehrabad, under the control of No. 74 Squadron RAF stationed there. No. 74 Squadron was stationed in Iran to repel any infiltration by the German forces that were advancing through the Caucasus in an attempt to reach the Persian oilfields in the south. A maintenance record contained an interesting note in Farsi indicated that at least one of the Mercury-powered Furies was equipped with a replacement tail wheel from a Hawker Hurricane.

The last known existing Persian Fury was located at Habbaniyah airbase in Iraq in 1948, where its engineless hulk was used for to train the station's fire-fighting crews. How that airplane ended up at that location is a mystery.

PERSIA BECOMES IRAN

On 21 March 1935, as part of Reza Shah's modernisation programme, the ancient name of Persia was changed to Iran. The Greeks had named the country Persia and the Shah wanted to emphasise the Aryan roots of Iran. The Persian State Department sent a telegram to all countries around the world, requesting all nations to use the name of Iran as the official name of the country formerly known as Persia.

As a result, the Persian Army Air Corps was renamed as the Imperial Iranian Air Force (IIAF) by military order No. 2366. The IIAF remained under the administration of the inspector general of aviation, who was one of seven inspectors serving under the Army chief-of-staff, until 1955 when the IIAF was separated from the Army and became an independent force. Until 21 March, PAAC personnel used Army uniforms and rank markings. However, a new blue uniform and emblem were created for the IIAF and these were issued to all personnel.

Hawker Fury Mk.II, serial 221, powered by a Bristol Mercury VISP-II engine, was one of the last batch of 12 Furies delivered to the PAAC in January 1935. (The Fabulous 30s)

The revised emblem of the PAAC in 1935, just before Persia was renamed Iran, which resulted in replacing the star on the top with an Imperial crown. The emblem once again was redesigned in 1955, when the IIAF became an independent force and remained unchanged until the 1979 Islamic Revolution. (History of IIAF)

Assembly of first batch of Hawker Audaxes with Hornet engines at Ahvaz. The RAF engineers supervised the assembly process performed by Iranian personnel, and test flew each aircraft before transferring them to Tehran. (History of IIAF)

HAWKER AUDAX

Built by the H.G. Hawker Engineering Co. (Hawker Aircraft Co. after July 1933), the Audax was a two-seat army cooperation aircraft bearing a marked resemblance to the Hawker Hart from which it evolved. Persia was one of the six air forces that purchased the Audax.

Between January 1934 and July 1935, Persia received total of 56 Hawker Audaxes in two batches. The first batch of 14 was ordered in March 1933 under contract No-389426/33. However, in order to compensate for the reduction of the number of Hawker Furies in the first order (as mentioned before), four aircraft were added to the Audax order, bringing the total of aircraft in the first order to 18.

In a situation similar to that with the Fury, the first batch of Hawker Audaxes was powered by the American-built 750hp Pratt & Whitney S2B1-G Hornet radial engine driving a three-blade Hamilton Standard Hydromatic metal propeller.

Hawker Audax 401, the first aircraft destined for Persia, made its maiden flight on 22 August 1933 at Brooklands, England. The initial tests with the Hornet engine revealed some problems, similar to those of the Furies. Aside from overheating, the American-built engine proved to be problematic due to its complicated cooling shutter arrangement in front of the cylinders, which was found to be unreliable. This resulted in a considerable engine life reduction in tropical climates and these engines therefore discarded. Also, the

Hawker Audax, serial 412, powered by a Pratt & Whitney S2B1-G Hornet engine, was the twelfth airplane from the first batch of 18 which was delivered in January 1934. (Aeroplane via Charles Sims)

nose heaviness caused by the heavy weight of the Hornet engine resulted in many taxiing accidents.

To evaluate the Hornet engine performance with a lighter overall weight, some tests were conducted with two-bladed Watts propellers. However, the two-blade wooden propeller proved to be underpowered and inadequate for the American engine.

The crated aircraft arrived at the port of Khoramshahr in January of 1934. From there they were transported by rail to Ahvaz for assembly and testing. The Audaxes then flew on to Tehran to join the 1st Air Regiment, wearing the serials 401 to 418.

The second batch of 12 aircraft were also powered by Hornet engines. These were originally intended to power the first batch of Persian Furies. The aircraft arrived during the months of November and December of 1934 and were assigned serials 419 to 430.

In order to alleviate problems with the Hornet-powered aircraft, Hawker suggested testing the aircraft with lighter British-built Bristol Pegasus engines. This option proved to be a good solution. As a result, the third batch of 26 aircraft, with serials 431 to 456, was fitted with the Pegasus engine. Known as the Pegasus Audax, these aircraft were ordered under contract No-406498/33 and were delivered between 1934 and 1935.

The first 10 aircraft of this batch of 26 Audaxes, were equipped with the Bristol Pegasus Mk-IIM engine, while the next 16 received the uprated Pegasus Mk-IIM2 engine. Both engines used the two-bladed Watts wooden propeller. The first six aircraft delivered were also equipped with dual controls for advanced combat training. Four others were geared for target towing for gunnery practice.

The last batch of Audaxes were 10 Bristol Mk.IIM2 Pegasus-powered aircraft assembled by the Shahbaz State Factory. Here they are warming up their engines for a training flight. The aircraft in the foreground is 458, identifying it as one of the Shahbaz-assembled airframes. (History of IIAF)

Hawker Audax, serial 450, from the fourth batch delivered, powered by a Bristol Pegasus engine and a 2-blade Watts wooden propeller. (Flight via John Yoxall)

Table 12: List of Hawker Audaxes delivered to Iran

Type	Engine	Qty	IIAF Serial	Manufacturer	Delivery
Hornet Audax	PW S2B1-G, Hornet	18	401–418	Hawker	January 1934
Hornet Audax	PW S2B1-G, Hornet	12	419–430	Hawker	November–December 1934
Pegasus Audax	Bristol Mk.IIM Pegasus	10	431–440	Hawker	March 1935
Pegasus Audax	Bristol Mk.IIM2 Pegasus	16	441–456	Hawker	July 1935
Shahdaxes	Hornet > Pegasus	5	457–461	Shahbaz	March 1938
Shahdaxes	Hornet > Pegasus	5	462–466	Shahbaz	March–April 1939

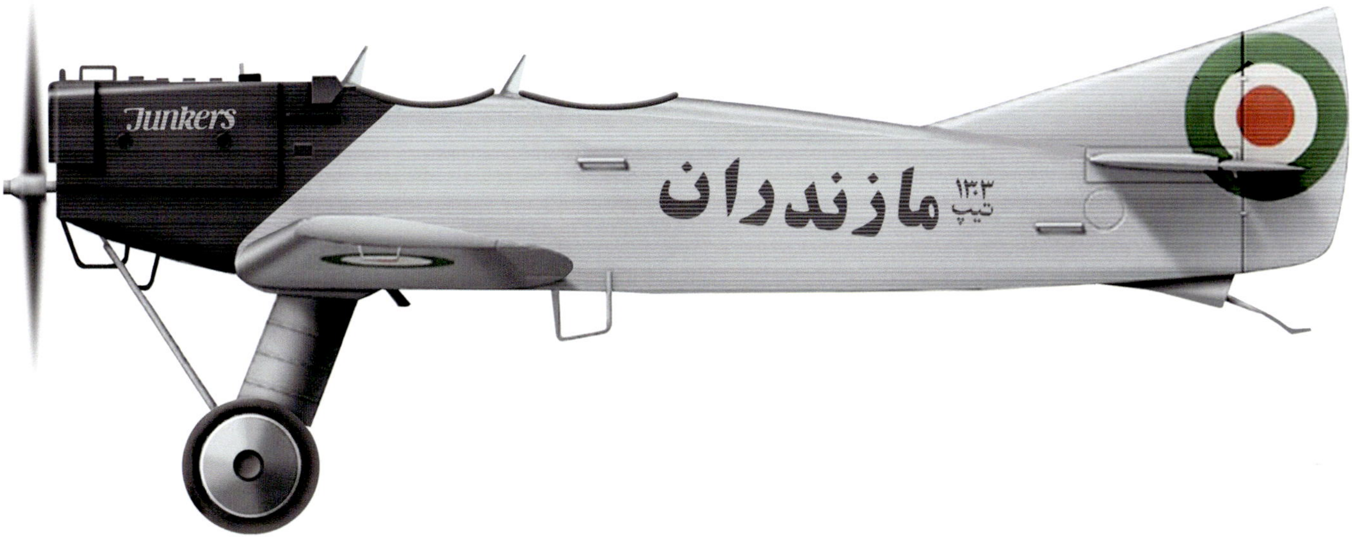

The Russian-assembled Polikarpov R-2, was purchased by donations collected from the people of the Mazandaran province, accordingly, it was named *Mazandaran* and was assigned to its Northern Brigade. Two other German-assembled A 20s also served in the Persian Army Air Corps in 1924. (Artwork by Leon Manouchehrians)

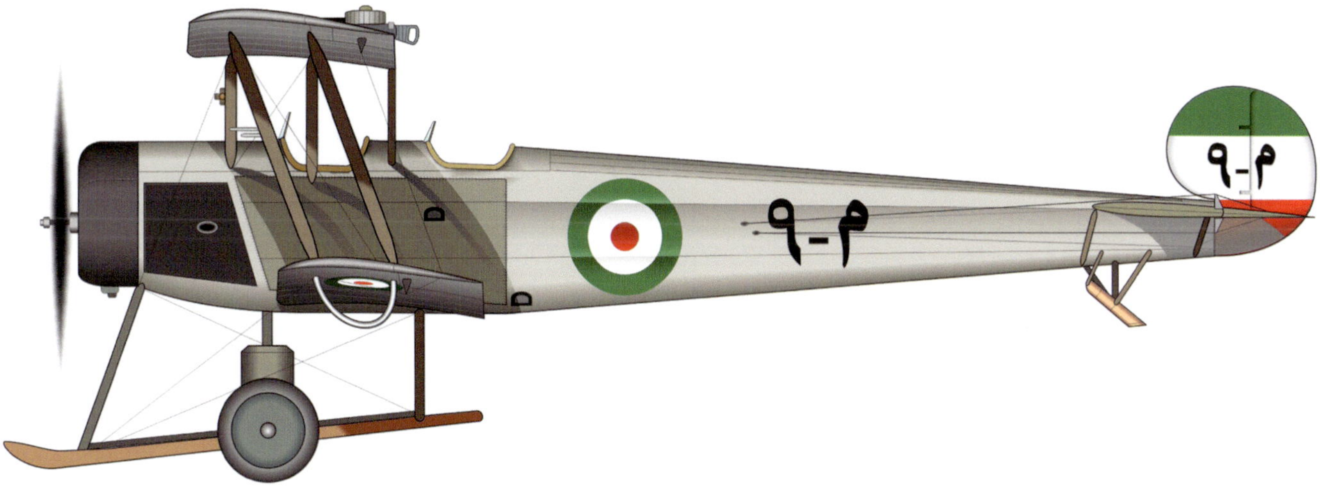

Polikarpov U-1 with Serial M9 was one of nine U-1s, which entered service with the Persian Army Air Corps. The U-1 was the license-built copy of the British Avro 504K, produced by Polikarpov at its Fili plant near Moscow. It was visually identical to its British original. While it was primarily considered as a trainer, it was used as a light bomber and observation aircraft during the Persian Civil War. (Artwork by Leon Manouchehrians)

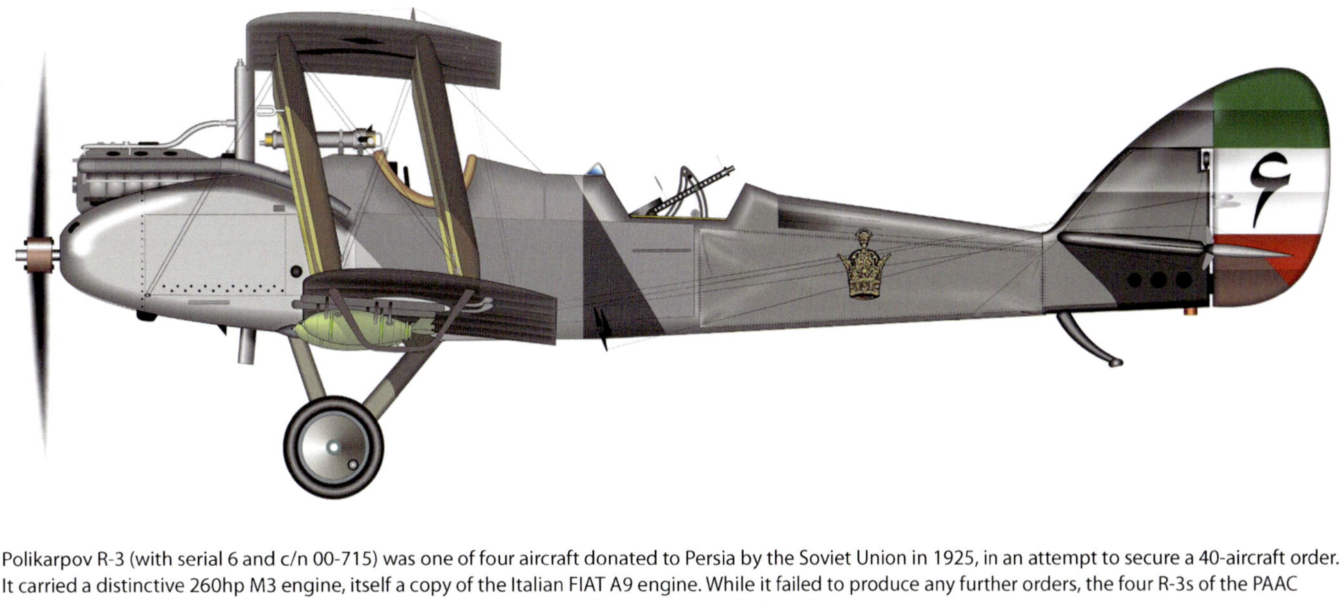

Polikarpov R-3 (with serial 6 and c/n 00-715) was one of four aircraft donated to Persia by the Soviet Union in 1925, in an attempt to secure a 40-aircraft order. It carried a distinctive 260hp M3 engine, itself a copy of the Italian FIAT A9 engine. While it failed to produce any further orders, the four R-3s of the PAAC rendered a magnificent service during the Persian Civil War. (Artwork by Leon Manouchehrians)

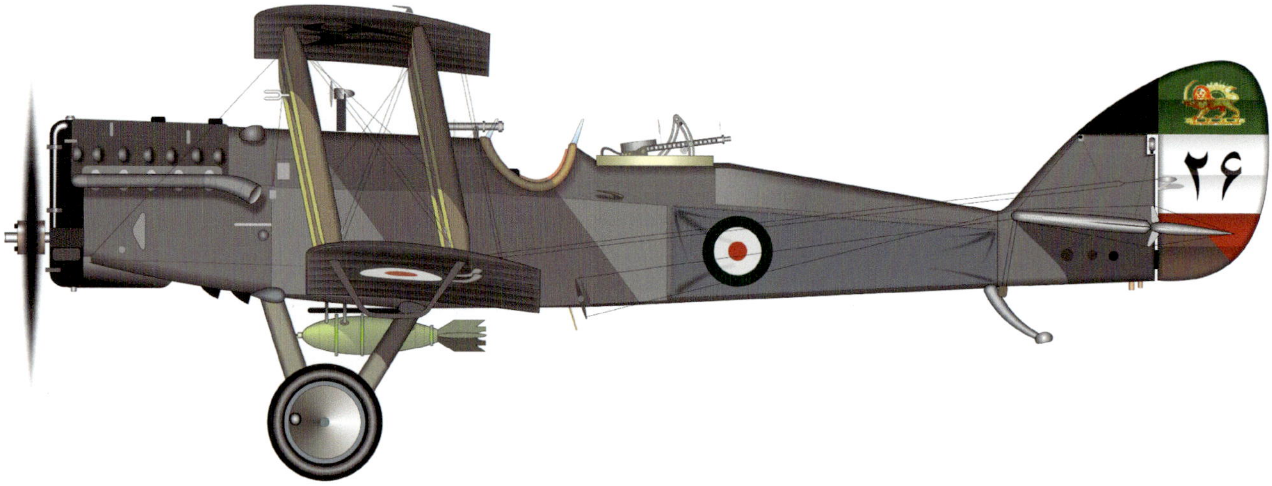

The Polikarpov R-1 was a license-built variant of the British de Havilland DH.9A and the backbone of the Persian Army Air Corps in the 1920s. No fewer than 27 were delivered, serving in all four regiments and participating in all military operations against rebellious tribes across Persia. The aircraft was used as fighter, bomber, and reconnaissance aircraft. Shown is aircraft 26, armed with Krupp bombs and machine guns. (Artwork by Leon Manouchehrians)

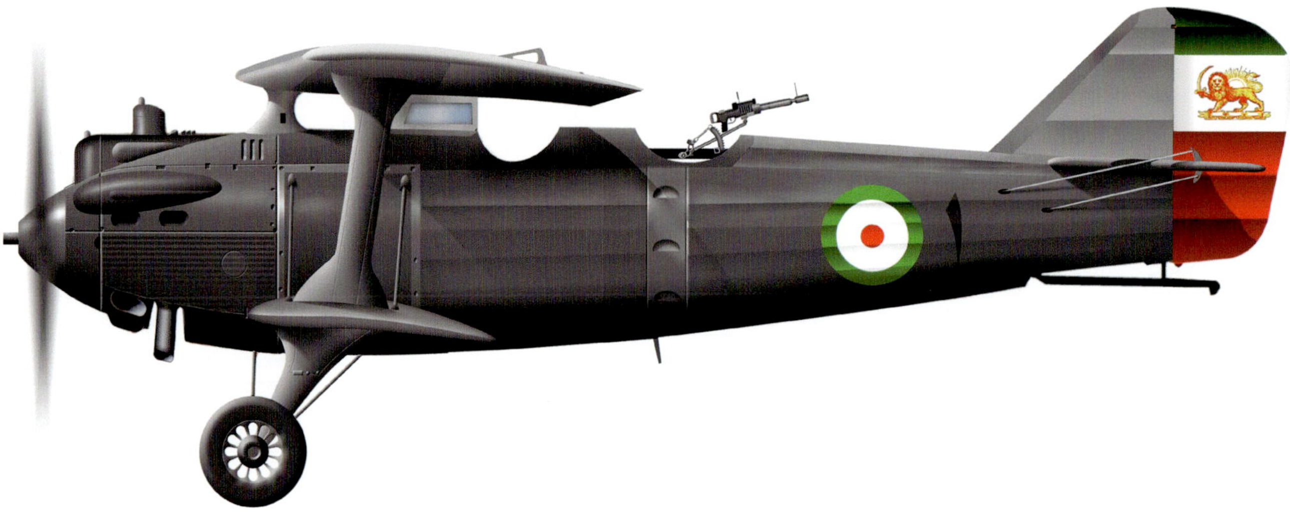

Persia received a single Breguet 19 A.2 reconnaissance variant. It was flown from Paris to Tehran by newly-graduated Persian aviator Colonel Ahmad Nakhjivan. His airplane was damaged during a landing at a muddy strip in Turkey. France provided another Bre. 19 A.2, enabling him to reach Tehran. For his daring attempt with only 200 hours of flying experience, Reza Shah promoted him as the first commander of the Persian Air Force. (Artwork by Leon Manouchehrians)

The Hawker Fury was the first British-built aircraft in Persian service and ordered in two batches of 12. Fury Mk.I serial 203 was one of six aircraft of the first batch of the first order, which were powered by American Pratt & Whitney S2B1-G Hornet engines. Due to problems with overheating in the Persian hot-and-high environment, the second batch was powered by the British Bristol Mercury VISP engine. (Artwork by Leon Manouchehrians)

Hawker Fury Mk.II serial 216 was of the second order of 12 delivered in 1935. Thanks to the satisfactory performance of the Bristol Mercury engine of the Mk.I in the Iranian climate, the Fury Mk.IIs were powered by uprated Bristol Mercury VISP-II engines. They received serials 213 to 224. The Fury was a single-seat fighter armed with machine guns. They served in all four regiments, carrying out combat missions against rebellious tribes. (Artwork by Leon Manouchehrians)

The Hawker Audax was the main fighter-bomber of the PAAC during the 1930s. Between 1934 and 1938, a total of 56 Audaxes were delivered in four batches. The first two batches of 18 and 12 were powered by PW S2B1-G Hornet engines. As was the case with the Hawker Furies, the American engine did not perform satisfactorily, and as a result some were returned to the UK for retrofitting these with the British Pegasus engine. Audaxes were involved on all fronts against separatist tribes. (Artwork by Leon Manouchehrians)

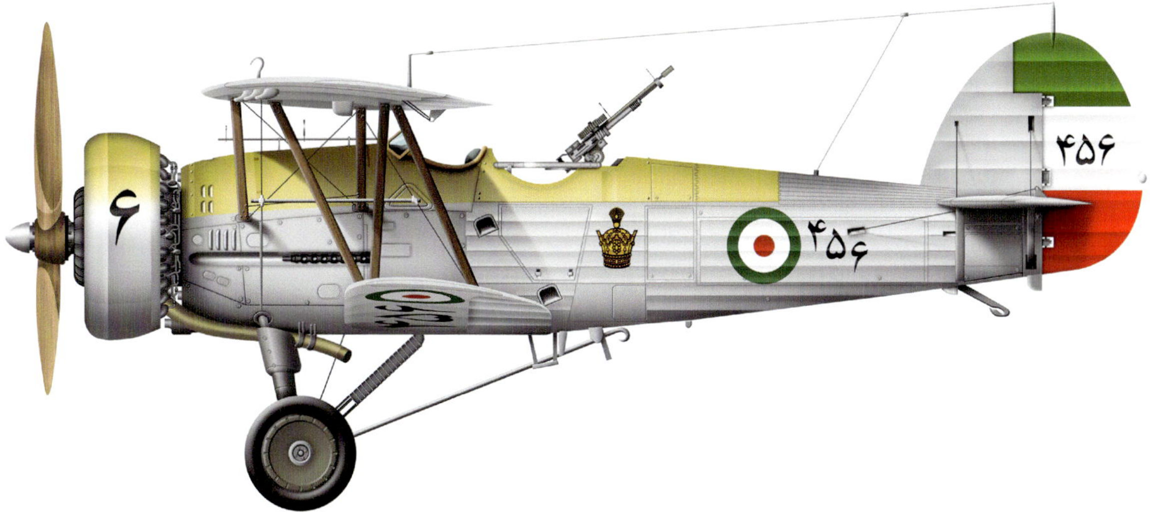

The third batch of 10 and fourth batch of 16 Audaxes were powered by Bristol Pegasus Mk.IIM and Mk.IIM2 engines respectively. Aircraft 456, deployed to Abadan in Iran, became famous when it effectively engaged with RAF Hurricanes and disrupted their bombing raid during the 1941 invasion by Allied forces. It survived the Second World War and served as a trainer at the Mehrabad pilot school, Tehran. (Artwork by Leon Manouchehrians)

Persia ordered 35 two-seat Hawker Hind trainers in 1935. During the late 1930s they were used as bomber / reconnaissance aircraft. Four aircraft were fitted with a focal lens camera installed in the rear cockpit on the machine gun scarf ring. During the 1946 Azerbaijan crisis, no fewer than 15 Hinds were still flying alongside the Hawker Hurricanes. Another 16 aircraft flew as trainers at the Mehrabad training academy until 1952. (Artwork by Leon Manouchehrians)

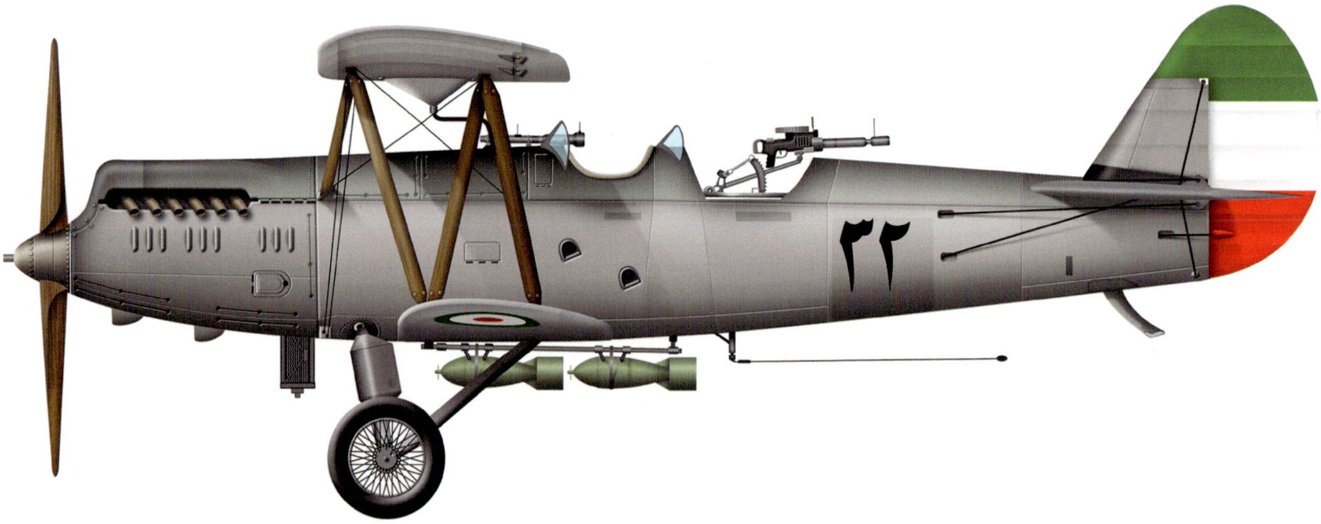

The Polikarpov R-5 was a reconnaissance-bomber specifically designed and built for the Soviet Air Force. Three Russian R-5s visited Tehran during the Great Eastern Tour, which was organised by Polikarpov to promote the type. After a competition with the French Potez 25, Persia ordered 10 R-5s. Able to carry an impressive load of bombs, they were effectively used during the Persian Civil War against rebellious tribes. (Artwork by Leon Manouchehrians)

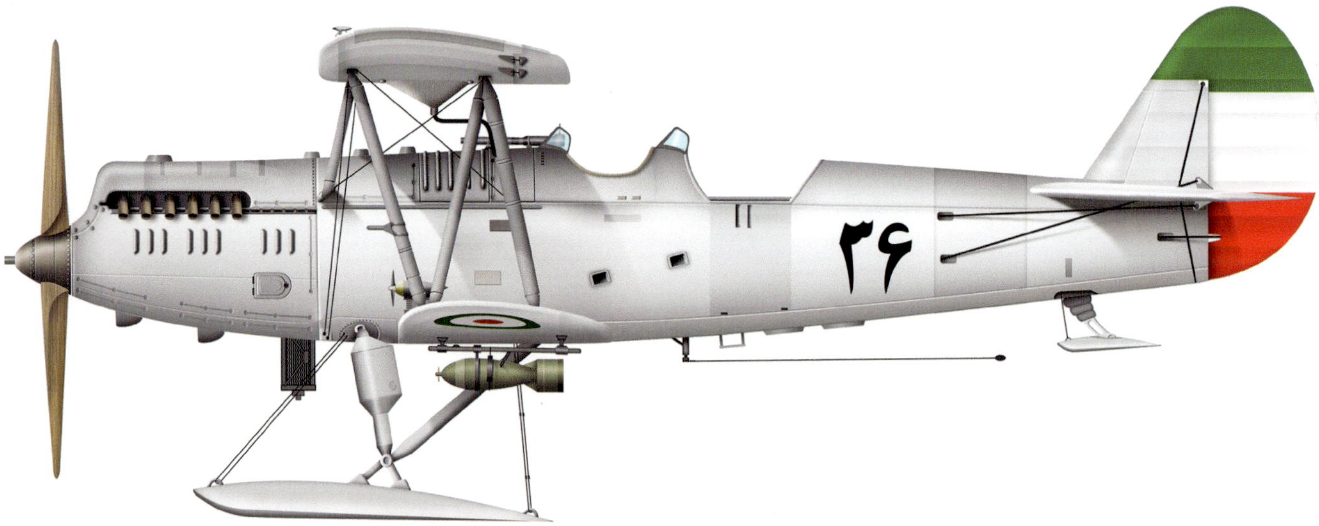

The Polikarpov R-5K was the ski-equipped variant of the type. Two of the 10 Persian R-5s delivered to the PAAC were equipped with skis. Overall white aircraft 36 was used in the north-eastern province of Khorasan and north-western province of Azerbaijan, where they had snow five to six months of the year. The ski-equipped R-5s could carry eight 50lb bombs. (Artwork by Leon Manouchehrians)

The Turkish-assembled Curtiss N2C-1 (serial 1401 and BuNo A8026) was a gift from the Government of Turkey to the Government of Iran to further strengthen relations between the two countries. It was flown from Turkey to Iran by German pilot Schwartz Etucer, who was a member of the German military attaché team in Turkey. The aircraft was transferred to the air force by order of Reza Shah. (Artwork by Leon Manouchehrians)

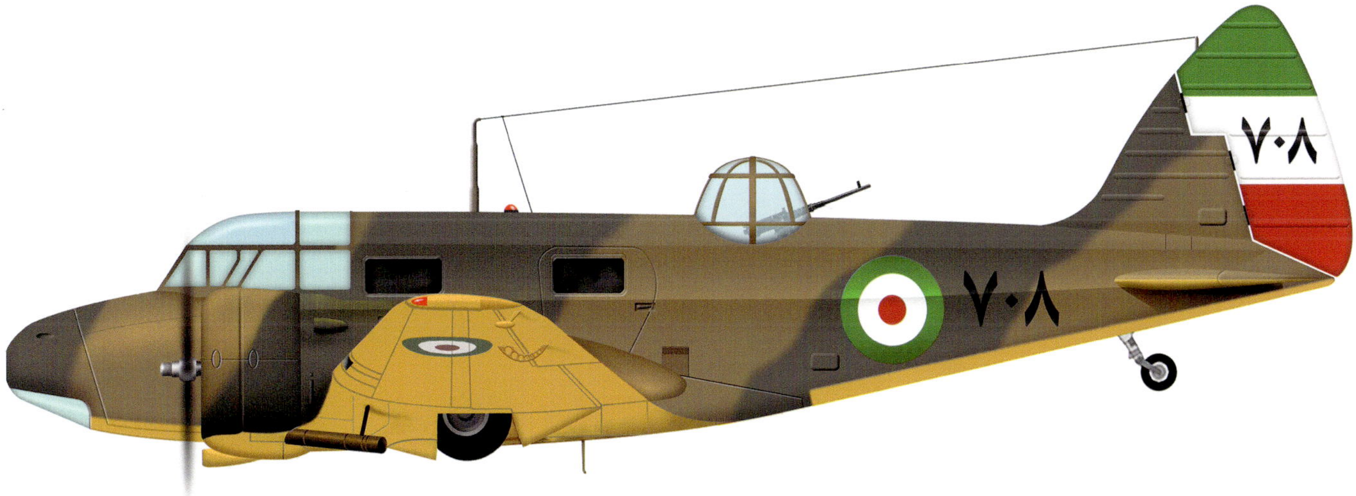

Three ex-Royal Air Force Airspeed AS.10 Oxfords were supplied to Iran just before the start of the Second World War. Equipped with a rooftop machine gun turret, they were used primarily as navigation and multi-engine trainers. They were later used as paradropping military transport aircraft after the Army airborne division was established. (Artwork by Leon Manouchehrians)

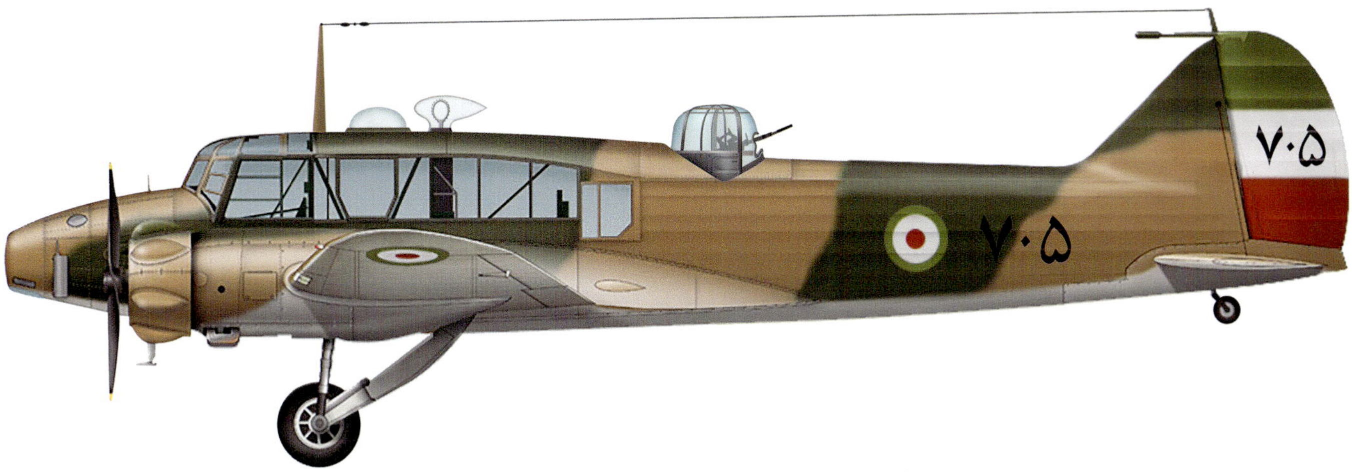

Following the end of the Second World War, Iran received 48 Avro Anson Mk.Is in 1946. They were delivered as compensation for several unfulfilled orders, as well as recognition for Iran's efforts towards the victory of the Allies. Iranian Ansons carried standard RAF Bomber Command camouflage. Aside from its primary role as a navigation trainer, they were extensively used as transport, bomber, and reconnaissance aircraft during the Azerbaijan and Kurdistan crisis. (Artwork by Leon Manouchehrians)

Between 1932 and 1940, 99 de Havilland DH.82 and DH.82A trainers were delivered in 11 batches to the Imperial Iranian Air Force, plus 10 more were assembled by the Shahbaz State Factory at Dowshan Tappeh airfield, bringing the total of Tiger Moths in Iranian service to 109. Six were fitted with covered cockpits for 'blind training'. Their secondary tasks were light bombing, reconnaissance, observation and liaison. (Artwork by Leon Manouchehrians)

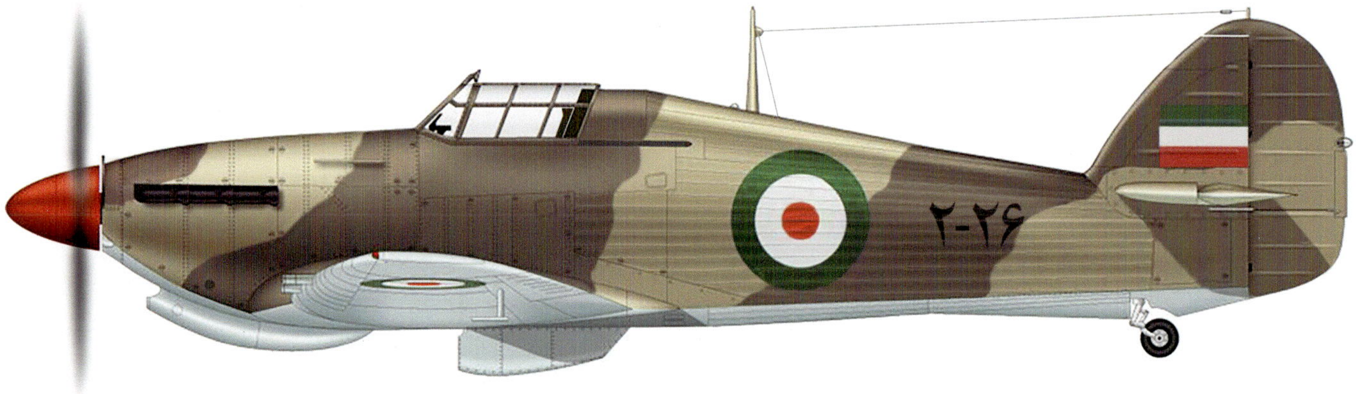

After the end of the Second World War, Britain finally delivered the long overdue 16 Hawker Hurricane Mk.IICs fitted with tropical filters. They were used as trainers since their four cannons were removed and their ports were plugged. They carried standard desert camouflage of the RAF with two-tone brown/sand overall, light pale blue undersides and red spinners. They were supplemented by 10 more Mk.IICs transferred from RAF 74 Squadron, stationed in Tehran. (Artwork by Leon Manouchehrians)

The Iranian Air Force received two two-seat Hawker Hurricane TMk.IICs trainers uniquely modified from two ex-RAF single-seat Mk.IIBs by adding a second cockpit behind the original one. Aside from a single example of another modified two-seat Hurricane supplied to the Soviet Air Force, no other two-seat Hurricane was ever delivered to any other air force. The overall white two seaters carried the 2-31 and 2-32 serial. (Artwork by Leon Manouchehrians)

Allied Invasion Routes (25–29 August 1941). (Map by Leon Manouchehrians)

Persian Gulf Command delivery routes. (Map by Leon Manouchehrians)

Iran in 1936 – Overview of IIAF bases and detachments in the various provinces. (Map by Leon Manouchehrians)

In late 1934, 10 out of 30 Hornet-powered Audaxes were sent back to Brooklands for engine conversion to the Pegasus. The final Audax, No 456, was first flown on 20 March 1935.

By late 1935, all 56 aircraft had been delivered to the recently renamed Imperial Iranian Air Force, forming 10 fighter squadrons equipped with the Audax, including 36 aircraft (14 Hornet and 22 Pegasus-powered) with the 1st Regiment at Tehran, 10 aircraft (six Hornets and four Pegasus) with the 2nd Regiment at Tabriz, six aircraft (Pegasus) with the 3rd Regiment at Mashhad and four aircraft (Pegasus) with the 4th Regiment at Ahvaz. In addition, a detachment of 10 Hornet-powered Audaxes from all four regiments served under the RAF Near East Command at Abadan airport.

All Iranian Audaxes were armed with a synchronised, fixed forward-firing 0.303in. (7.7mm) Vickers Mk-III or Mk-V machine gun, a Lewis machine gun of the same calibre on the rear cockpit pivoting scarf, with five 97-round ammunition drums and underwing bomb racks with up to eight 20lb bombs. In addition to these weapons, 20lb (9kg) or 112lb (51kg) desert store-supply containers could also be carried on the bomb racks.

The Audax was the first Persian fighter aircraft to be equipped with radio communication. The test was carried out when on 18 August 1934 Hawker Audax No. 412, fitted with an American RCA model AVR-15A radio receiver, flown by 1st Lieutenant Gholamhossein Mostafavi, took off from Ghaleh Morghi airfield.

Escorted by two other Audaxes, he flew a triangular route between Tehran, Sultan Abad, and Khoramabad, with a short refuelling stop at Sultan Abad. The flight lasted three hours and 35 minutes. All three aircraft landed at Ghaleh Morghi at 1740hrs local time, and the pilot reported flawless communications. With successful test results between the aircraft and ground radio stations, most Iranian aircraft were subsequently fitted with radios.

Five additional Hawker Audaxes, initially powered by Hornets but later re-engined with the Bristol Pegasus, were assembled by the Shahbaz State Factory around March 1938. This was followed by five more in March and April 1939 from components supplied by Hawker from Great Britain. These aircraft received serial numbers 457 to 466.

The Shahbaz-assembled Audaxes, called 'Shahdaxes' (combination of Shahbaz and Audax), were inspected by Reza Shah and the Crown Prince Mohammad Reza on 23 July 1938 at Dowshan Tappeh airfield where the factory was located. The 10 Shahdaxes flew in an impressive formation flight. Reza Shah expressed his satisfaction and gratitude to Colonel Nakhjivan, commander of the IIAF, and for the first time to the British Ambassador and the military attaché for the erection of the aircraft assembly factory by the British government and the technical support of the Royal Air Force.

During their service Iranian Audaxes visited Turkey and Egypt in 1934 and 1938 respectively. The Turkish deployment was intended to reinforce political, economic and military cooperation between the two countries following the Reza Shah's visit to Turkey in 1934.

Five Hornet-powered Audaxes under the command of Captain Mostafa Yaftabadi, took off at 0930 hours on 23 October 1934 from Ghaleh Morghi airfield and flew to Ankara via Tabriz and Eskisir. They entered Turkish airspace after receiving prior authorisation by telegram from the Turkish government.

Using their basic compass for navigation and ground maps for visual references, the five Iranian Audaxes reached Ankara after nearly 13 hours of flight. There, a large crowd of officials and public were awaiting at the airport to welcome the Iranian aircraft and its crew. A group of 18 personnel, including five reserve pilots, three observers and 10 mechanics along with some spare parts, had arrived two days earlier by train to support the deployment.

1st Lieutenant Gholamhossein Mostafavi (left) in front of radio-equipped Audax 412 and two other pilots who flew with him on the first radio-check flight on 18 August 1934. (History of IIAF)

Reza Shah inspects the 10 Shahbaz-assembled Audaxes during their delivery ceremony on 23 July 1938 at Dowshan Tappeh airfield where the factory was located. Crown Prince Mohammad Reza and IIAF commander Colonel Nakhjivan accompany the Shah. (INA)

Hornet-powered Audaxes ready for take-off on a combat mission from a desert airstrip near Isfahan. (AELR)

Reza Shah, with Colonel Nakhjivan on his left and Crown Prince Mohammad Reza behind him, inspect the Shahbaz-assembled Audaxes at Dowshan Tappeh. The first aircraft is 461. (AKTA)

The Iranian group stayed in Turkey for 15 days. Aside from visiting various facilities and historical sites, they conducted joint exercises with the Turkish Air Force to gain experience in long distance deployment. The five Audaxes flew 131 hours and 29 minutes during the visit. The Turkish visit marked the first official deployment of Iranian military aircraft outside the country, flown by an all-Iranian crew and participated in joint military manoeuvres.

When Allied forces invaded Iran in August 1941, no fewer than 20 Audaxes were still in active Iranian service. Royal Air Force Hawker Hurricanes and Gloster Gladiators downed six Iranian Audaxes in dogfights over Bandar-e-Shahpur, Haftkel, and Khaneghin. In addition, they destroyed more on the ground, with one destroyed at Abadan airport and three others at Ahvaz airport.

With the arrival of the Hawker Hinds, most of the Audaxes were reassigned to the 4th Regiment at Ahvaz. One or two survived the Second World War, only to be scrapped when surplus aircraft became available after the war at low prices. The last Iranian Audax was taken out of service in June 1946.

Nine of the Persian pilots before deployment to Mashhad on an army support mission. From the left: Captains Ghalehyee, Minayee, Zanganeh, Garisi, Moyeeni, Imany, Vaseghi, Tajvari, and Zande-Moghadam. (History of IIAF)

Captain Mostafa Yaftabadi was the leader of five Hornet-powered Audaxes which visited Turkey on 23 October 1934. The formation flew most of the route under visual rules and compass navigation. (aerospacetalk.ir)

Commemorative photograph of Persian pilots and mechanics with Turkish personnel, including the base and host squadron commanders as well as foreign military attachés in front of a Persian Audax with its engine covered. (IIAF archive)

THE MISSING AUDAXES

In response to the *Iranian Eagles* article by Swedish aviation historian and author Lennart Andersson in Air Enthusiast magazine (March/April 2001), Vladimir Kotelinkov from Moscow, Russia, made the following comment:

During the course of the Soviet-British occupation of Iran in August 1941, several Iranian aircraft were not only captured, but also were later used in service by the Soviet Union.

Starting from 1 July 1942, the service lists of the Armenian Independent Detachment of the GVF (Civil Air Fleet) recorded a "Hort" aircraft. This fact awoke my interest, and looking through another document I found this under designation "Hawker Hart". The aircraft was in service in Armenia for more than two years and was flown by various pilots: M. Paraksheev, B. Vozdyakov, G. Mouradyan and V. Ovsepyan. In 1943, a similar Hart appeared in the Georgian Department of the GVF. The aircraft was delivered from workshop 33 in Tbilisi and noted as "restored" and was flown by P. Ustinov.

Both Harts were documented as "delivered to GVF from the VVS RKKA (Air Force of the Workers-Peasants of the Red Army)". Originally, I thought that it had been aircraft evacuated from Baltic States in summer of 1941.

According to the report by Major General Sinyakov, made on 25 August 1940 in Riga, when USSR annexed the Baltic States, the VVS RKKA took into its possession of ten serviceable aircraft of the Hart type in total (seven Harts in Estonia and three Hinds in Latvia).

But checking through the serial number lists of the engines, I found that Georgian and Armenian biplanes had American Pratt & Whitney Hornet S2B1-G engines. For aircraft of the Hart family, such engines were installed only on Audaxes of the first Iranian order (30 aircraft) delivered in 1933-34.

These Audaxes, marked as Harts by error, were probably captured in 1941 by the units of 44th Soviet Army in Tabriz, Iran, where almost all aircraft of the 2nd Iranian Regiment were taken by Soviet forces. Alternatively, it could be the equipment of the 3rd Regiment taken in Mashhad. According to another report, at least one aircraft was still in Yerevan, Armenia in February 1945. Starting May 1945, the "Harts" disappeared in the lists of the GVF".

In response to Vladimir Kotelnikov's note Lennart Andersson added:

The Aeroflot Audaxes were registered CCCP-L192 and CCCP-L193 as Hawker Harts. The construction numbers of these aircraft were entered in the registry as 61/41861, and 61/E-1261 respectively. The first machine was used by GVF's Georgian Department and the second by the Armenian Detachment.

Just as Mr. Kotelnikov did at first, I thought that these machines were Estonian Harts taken in 1940, but I could not find an explanation for the construction numbers. The number '418' is of course the Iranian serial number. 'E-12' is more difficult to explain. It could perhaps be a number assigned by the repair shop.

By December 1943 the following Hornet-engined IIAF Audaxes were "missing": 411, 413, 416, 418, 419, 420, 422, 426, 427, 428, and 429. At least six of these had crashed before 1939. The total number of IIAF Audaxes decreased by some 20 between November 1939 and December 1942 and it seems likely that a portion of these were actually taken by Soviet forces in 1941 and were turned over to VVS.

HAWKER HIND

The Hawker Hind two-seat light bomber was produced to meet Air Ministry Specification G.7/34 for an interim replacement for the Hart. Thus, the Hind became the last biplane light bomber of the RAF. Minor refinements in the Hind included a tail wheel in place of a skid, 'ram-horn' exhaust manifolds and the angled cut out of the rear cockpit to improve the field of fire for the gunner. Being a dual-control aircraft, the Hind was also considered to be used as an advanced operational trainer. It was also used for gunnery training. Following the successful introduction of the Audax and Fury, the Iranian government ordered 35 Hawker Hinds in 1935 receiving serials 601–635, powered by 575hp Bristol Mercury VIII engines.

First of 35 Hawker Hinds for Iran, serial 601, powered by a Bristol Mercury VIII engine, photographed during test flights at Brooklands, UK. (Hawker)

The first aircraft, No.601, was flown by Hawker chief test pilot P.G. Lucas on 28 April 1935. As with most aircraft of that period, test flights revealed persistent engine overheating problems, which were only cured by improvements to the engine cooling system, such as the addition of water bulges around the cowling and limiting the engine running speed.

The first batch of 18 was delivered in July 1935 and the second batch of 17 arrived in January 1939. Starting in February 1939, 20 more Hinds were built by the Shahbaz State Factory, all of which were delivered by the spring of 1941.

Four Hinds were assigned aerial photography tasks for which they were fitted with large format Zeiss-Humber 23-44 focal cameras with a 117mm Lucas lens in the rear cockpit. The reconnaissance Hinds were effectively used during the third segment of the Iranian civil war by photographing the positions and hideouts of the Bakhtiari and Bassery nomads in the south, Turk and Azeri separatists in the north, and rioting Baluch and Ghashghayi tribes in central Iran, just before the start of the Second World War.

In anticipation of introducing the Hawker Hinds into Iranian service, in 1934 Captain Mehdi Sepahpour (later Lieutenant General and commander of the IIAF 1948–1951) was sent to Great Britain for advanced reconnaissance and photo-interpretation training. He later returned to England for additional training in tactical reconnaissance when he was attached to RAF Hemswell as a foreign officer from 24 August to 6 September 1938. Forming two squadrons within the four regiments, Iranian Hinds were also used as bombers during 1938–39 operations against armed Al-Ahvaz Arab nomads in Fars and Khuzestan provinces.

A Hawker test pilot gets on board Iranian Hind serial 631 at Brooklands, UK. All 35 Hinds were test flown by Hawker pilots before they were disassembled and crated for shipment to Iran. (A.J. Jackson collection)

Hind 611 was one of four aircraft that were fitted with a Zeiss-Humber 23-44 focal camera in the rear cockpit. The machine gun rack, used for the camera, allowed the photo-observer to tilt the camera downwards at a 55-degree angle. (Imperial Aeroclub)

Detachment of Hawker Hinds from 1st and 2nd Regiments based at Ahvaz in 1939 for operations against Al-Ahvaz Arab nomads, just before start of the Second World War. Note the covered RAF Bristol Blenheim parked in the back row between IIAF Hinds. (Author's collection)

During the Second World War, training detachments, with two Hinds each, were formed at Abadan, Boushehr, Aghajari and Shiraz, while 16 Hinds were permanently stationed at the main training centre at Tehran's Mehrabad airbase.

During the 1946 Azerbaijan crisis, no fewer than 15 Hinds were still flying alongside the Hawker Hurricanes. Twin Lewis machine guns installed in the rear cockpit of Hinds were used to strafe ground targets while the aircraft circled in bank position over the target. The Hawker Hind remained in Persian service until the 1950s. The last three Hinds of the Mehrabad Training school were withdrawn from service in 1952, when the delivery of a large number of T-6 Texans to the IIAF was completed.

Close-up of a twin Lewis machine gun in the rear cockpit of Hawker Hind. Not all Iranian Hinds were armed with machine guns. A few used the same rack to install a reconnaissance camera and few were dual-control aircraft with flight instruments in the rear cockpit for use as trainer. (Air Pictorial)

1930s MILITARY EXERCISES

Organised by the 4th Army Battalion stationed at Tabriz, the first full scale military exercises by the Imperial Iranian Air Force commenced on 8 September 1935 and ended 13 days later. During this series of exercises, 11 participating aircraft departed from the 1st Regiment base at Ghaleh Morghi, Tehran, and flew to Tabriz, in the north-western part of Iran, to practice air support of army units.

The deployed squadron consisted of three Hawker Audaxes, four Hawker Furies and four Hawker Hinds, all flown by high-ranking officers including Belgian Colonel Victor Bevir, who was commanding the operation.

The next set of exercises with large participation of the air force occurred on 6 May 1939, when 19 Hawker Hinds, 28 Tiger Moths, 11 Hawker Furies and 14 Hawker Audaxes were deployed to Khorasan, The observers carried out photo-reconnaissance missions, using the cameras installed on the Hinds.

During the deployment of any base squadron to a combat zone, a small back up unit, usually consisting of six to eight aircraft, was kept at full readiness at the same base. Here nine Hawker Hinds of the 3rd Fighter-Bomber Squadron of 1st Regiment at Ghaleh Morghi form a flight line with aircraft 615 in the foreground. (pond5-video frame)

Hawker Hind, serial 633, armed with a Lewis machine gun. Note the angled cut of the rear cockpit sides, compared to the Hawker Hart it originates from, which considerably improved the scope of downward fire of the machine gun. (Air Profiles #6)

5

PRELUDE TO THE SECOND WORLD WAR

Towards the end of the 1930s, six new aircraft types entered Iranian service, consisting of one Curtiss N2C Fledgling, one Praga E.114 Air Baby, one RWD-13, three de Havilland DH.89M Dragon Rapides, one Hawker Hurricane Mk.I, and three Airspeed AS.10 Oxfords.

The Curtiss N2C-1 was presented to Iran as a gift from the Turkish government to further strengthen the friendly relationship of the two countries following the visit of Reza Shah to Turkey. The E.114 and RWD-13 were presented as a gift from the governments of Czechoslovakia and Poland respectively for the occasion of the upcoming wedding of Crown Prince Mohammad Reza Pahlavi with Princess Fowzieh in 1939.

These three gifted aircraft entered service as private aircraft of the Crown Prince. However, as they were not used much by the monarchy, all three aircraft were ordered to be transferred to the air force after a short period of time. That was done due to the small number of aircraft in Iranian inventory after the invasion by Anglo-Soviet forces.

CURTISS N2C-1 FLEDGLING

Designated N2C-1, known internally to Curtiss as the Model 48, was a trainer aircraft developed for the United States Navy in the late 1920s.[1] In 1934, the first Turkish-assembled N2C-1 serial 1401, BuNo A8026, was flown from Turkey to Iran by German pilot Schwartz Etucer, who was a member of the German military attaché team in Turkey.[2] The pilot remained in Iran for two months to train 1st Lieutenant Morad Nikseresht.

After the transfer to the IIAF the aircraft received serial 2-60. The Iranian military expressed interest in the type and at one time announced plans to order 20 Fledglings for training, but with the start of the Second World War and the occupation of Iran by Allied forces in August 1941, this plan never materialised.

The N2C-1 was used as trainer. However, not much flying time was logged on this plane due to a shortage of spare parts and lack of trained ground crew to keep the plane airworthy. As a result, the sole Iranian Fledgling was grounded around 1944 and remained in storage at Ghaleh Morghi airfield until it was scrapped in 1951.

Curtiss N2C-1 serial 2-60 was a large training airplane. Originally donated to Iran for political goodwill, it was later transferred to the air force and was kept at Dowshan Tappeh for advanced training. (Abbas Atrvash)

The sole Persian N2C-1 at Tabriz. From left to right: French military attaché Monsieur Neli, 2nd Regiment vice commander Major Ghiujani, pilot 1st Lieutenant Morad Nikseresht, German pilot Schwartz Etucer, pilots Captain Kium and Captain Alayee. (IIAF archive)

Below: Turkish-assembled N2C-1, serial 1401 and BuNo A8026, was flown from Turkey to Iran by the German pilot Schwartz Etucer, who was a member of the German military attaché team in Turkey. (Russell T. Gerow collection)

PRAGA E.114 AIR BABY

The Praga E.114 was a single-engine sports airplane, designed by Jaroslav Slechta, and manufactured by the Czechoslovakian company C.K.D. Praga.[3] Due to its light weight, it was also called the Air Baby. Concerning C.K.D., Iran was not an unknown business partner, as in May 1935 Ceskomorayska-Kolben-Danek had received an order for the supply of 51 Praga AH-IV and 51 TNH light tanks to the Iranian army. The prototype of the Praga P-1 tank was also presented to the Reza Shah as a gift to strengthen the position of C.K.D. in future sales of military hardware to Iran.

E.114 Air Baby at Dowshan Tappeh. Standing first on the left is Czech pilot Lieutenant Jaroslav Polma, who flew the airplane from Prague to Tehran. (Marcel-Karet)

The E.114 (c/n 5) delivered to Iran was a former Czechoslovakian Air Force aircraft, powered by a 29kW (36hp) Aeronca air-cooled 'flat four' engine mounted in the extreme nose with its cylinders exposed. The Air Baby, registration OK-AZN, left Prague airport (in Czechoslovakia at the time) on 27 November 1938 with Lieutenant Jaroslav Polma at the controls.

According to Iranian archives, OK-AZN flew through Vienna, Budapest, Belgrade, Sofia, Istanbul, Ankara, Malatya, Diarbakir, Rezaiyeh, Zanjan, Qazvin, and landed at Dowshan Tappeh airport, Tehran, some eight days later. After a brief ceremony, the Czechoslovakian ambassador officially presented the aircraft to the Crown Prince on behalf of the Czechoslovakian government.

In December 1942, the E.114 was transferred to the IIAF and received serial 2-50. It was pressed into service with the composite squadron at Ghaleh Morghi, flying as an auxiliary liaison aircraft alongside Airspeed Oxfords and Hawker Hurricanes. In February 1945, the Praga E.114 was overhauled by engineers of the Skoda truck assembly plant in Tehran and was passed onto the Civil Aeroclub as EP-ACA for the training of Iranian air force pilots. The sole Iranian Air Baby was ultimately scrapped in 1948.

The sole E.114 with an Imperial crown on its fuselage inside a hangar at Dowshan Tappeh with Czech pilot Lieutenant Jaroslav Polma holding the prop as a mechanic works on the engine and a soldier guards the plane. (Marcel-Karet)

RWD-13

The RWD-13 was a touring plane, developed from the RWD-6 and RWD-9 sports planes. It was designed by Stanislaw Rogalski and Jerzy Drzewiecki of the RWD design bureau at the DWL (*Doswiadczalne Warsztaty Lotnicze*) workshops in Warsaw, Poland.[4]

The RWD-13 gifted to Iran was registered SP-BNY with c/n 285 and production line number DWL-22. The aircraft arrived at Tabriz airport on 6 April 1939 and flew after a short stay on to Tehran Ghaleh Morghi airfield where it was officially handed over to the military authorities. The Polish pilot who ferried the plane was Mscislaw Czerwinski. He stayed in Iran as a guest of the palace for three months to train two Iranian air force officers to fly it.

SP-BNY, destined for Iran, during an engine run test at the DWL workshop near Warsaw, Poland, before delivery with Polish pilot Mscislaw Czerwinski at the controls. (*Narodowe Archiwum Cyfrowe*)

Handover of the RWD-13 aircraft SP-BNY on behalf of the President of the Republic of Poland, Ignacy Mościcki, to the Crown Prince of Iran. Identified from left to right are: Polish pilot Stefan Kryński, Polish pilot Eugeniusz Przysiecki and his wife, special diplomatic envoy of Iran to Poland Hamid Sayyah, and Iranian state department diplomat Fereydoon Janparvar. (Narodowe Archiwum Cyfrowe)

The aircraft remained in the personal use of the Crown Prince, however, after its transfer to the air force its civil registration was changed to military serial 2-70. Due to lack of spare parts and proper maintenance, the aircraft was withdrawn from service and put into storage in 1944 and scrapped in 1947.

DH.89M DRAGON RAPIDE

Since the expiration of the contract with the Persian Junkers Company in 1933, the need for a new air transport system in Persia was evident. In 1936, Reza Shah ordered the Iranian Ministry of Post, Telegram and Telephone (PTT) to establish an air mail network, which would occasionally carry passengers between the capital city and the centres of the provinces. The search for a suitable aircraft began.

With the domination of Britain in Iranian affairs, it was no surprise that the British de Havilland DH.89 Dragon Rapide was selected. While three aircraft were purchased by the Ministry of War, they were operated by the PTT, albeit with military pilots and maintenance crew.

Almost immediately, two air force officers (Colonel Nezammedin Nafez, and Colonel Khanbaba Alla) were sent to England for pilot training on the Dragon Rapides. They joined Major Abolfath Afghami, who was already in England studying civil aviation and air transport management. On their return to Iran three months later, a contract was signed between the Iranian and Iraqi governments for a once-a-week airmail service between the two countries. The mentioned three officers flew to Baghdad with three Tiger Moths through Kermanshah and Ghasre-Shirin to evaluate the route and the airport facilities.

In June 1936, just about two weeks after their return from England, the three Dragon Rapides arrived in crates at the port of Khoramshahr. They were transported by rail and assembled at Ahvaz airport from where all three aircraft were test flown by Peter de Havilland, after which the three Iranian pilots flew the three Rapides to Tehran.

In addition to Colonel Nafez and Colonel Alla as pilots, Lieutenant Vaziri, Captain Sehhat, Captain Mohtedi and Captain Molaghati flew as radio operators, for the postal service to the centre of the provinces. Captain Satari and Corporal Ferdosi were in charge of maintenance and ground handling. From 1939, Colonel Sepahpour and 2nd Lieutenant Rad Farz also joined the two pilots flying the Dragon Rapides between Tehran and Baghdad.

The Allied invasion of August 1941 halted operations for a year, but it was restarted in 1942. The service remained active until 1948, when the air mail service was transferred to the newly established Iranian Airways.

General view of the three Iranian DH.89Ms at Hartfield in May 1936, showing the gun sight attached to the nose and extended dorsal fin. (Aeroplane)

The all-black Iranian DH.89M devoid of any markings or serials, had a non-standard white tail with extended dorsal fin. (Aeroplane)

The origin of these three aircraft, however, has been a story of mystery, intrigue and subterfuge. During the Spanish Civil War of 1936–39, the Western countries signed a non-intervention agreement which banned sale of any military hardware to Spain, including aircraft. To bypass international rules, arms dealers and aircraft buyers approached British companies between 1935 and 1938 to buy British aircraft in defiance of the ban. This included DH.89s.

Very few DH.89s have officially been acknowledged as having been sent to Spain during the civil war period. One example, registered EC-AZZ, had been in service with *Lineas Aereas Postales Espanoles*, the predecessor of Iberia, since November 1934, but this aircraft was merely a passenger and postal transport. In addition, the three well known Spanish DH.89Ms were officially intended 'for colonial police work in Spanish Morocco', so that these would not be subject to an export embargo. No other Rapides were officially involved.

In fact, despite British records of transfers to Spain indicating only the four aircraft mentioned above, it seems certain that as many as 20 DH.89s were caught up in the battle. To add more mystery, even de Havilland's order records are unclear, thanks to the intentionally circuitous purchasing methods of the secretive buyers. Available data shows that the three DH.89Ms produced in 1935, usually assumed to be those for the Moroccan Police (c/n 6321, 6322, and 6323), were actually sold to the government of Iran. On order forms it appears that these were not built as military models, rather as standard DH.89s. Contemporary reports indicate that they were sold to the Imperial Iranian War Ministry for use on internal postal and passenger routes from Tehran. However, inspection of the three aircraft would have revealed they were actually intended for offensive use.

The Iranian DH.89Ms were armed with a forward-firing Vickers 'F' fixed machine gun in the nose with a ring-and-bead gun sight in the cockpit. In addition, a message hook and bomb racks installed under the fuselage were capable of carrying twelve 271b bombs. Finally, a rear upper gun was provided with a scarf ring which could be detached and folded back into the cabin. The DH.89M, built to Air Ministry Specification G.18/35, was capable of carrying four stretchers.

Perhaps it would be appropriate to make a correction on the fate of the three Iranian Military Rapides. For many years and in many publications, it is mentioned erroneously that the three Iranian DH.89Ms were ultimately

Close-up views of Iranian DH.89M: from top to bottom: the nose-mounted Vickers 'F' fixed machine gun, a message hook and the bomb racks under the fuselage, capable of carrying 27lb bombs. (Aeroplane)

A curved retractable rack was installed on the rooftop to prevent the machine gun from firing at its own tail and stabiliser. (Aeroplane)

transferred to the Spanish Air Force as 40-1, 40-2, and 40-3. The truth is that these were three other earlier model aircraft with construction numbers 6310 (ex G-ADYK), 6311 (ex G-ADYL), and 6312 (ex G-ADYM). The reason for confusion might have been the fact that the three Spanish aircraft and the Iranian examples were identical in cabin configuration, armament fit, extended dorsal fin, and even black fuselage and white tail colours.

To keep their intended recipient unknown, the Iranian DH.89Ms had no national markings or serials. One of them, however, had a small Ministry of War title in Farsi painted on the port side passenger door. After the end of the Second World War and the Azerbaijan Crisis in 1946, the three DH.89Ms were transferred to the newly established State Airlines as EP-AAA (the very first Iranian aircraft with EP registrations), EP-AAB and EP-AAC.[5] Later in 1948 and 1949, they were sold back to the RAF where they became HK915, HK916 and HK917 respectively.[6]

HAWKER HURRICANE MK.I

Iran looked at the Hurricane with interest in 1937 when two RAF Mk.Is en route from Egypt to Burma arrived at the Shahbaz State Factory at Tehran's Dowshan Tappeh airbase for routine maintenance.

The Hurricane was considered the single-wing development of the Hawker Hind, with which Iran had considerable experience. The type was also recommended by RAF advisors in Iran as the best choice for a fighter-bomber, along with the Supermarine Spitfire for the air defence role.[7]

With the long relationship established between the Iranian government and the Hawker Company in the 1930s with Audax, Fury and Hind biplanes still serving in the Iranian air force, a letter of interest for the Hawker Hurricane was sent to Britain pending the evaluation of its performance in Iranian environments.

As a result, ex-RAF Hurricane Mk.I L2079 was sent to Iran for a six-month trial period on 28 July 1939. The aircraft arrived by container in the port of Boushehr on 27 August and was transported to Ahvaz by road, where it was assembled and flown to Tehran by Hawker test pilot Richard Reynell on 18 October.

Ex-RAF Hurricane Mk.I L2079 outside a hangar at Ghaleh Morghi airfield. Visible inside the hangar is one of the Iranian Airspeed Oxfords. (Captain Jahangir Salem)

Reza Shah and Crown Prince Mohammad Reza inspect the two newly-arrived Dragon Rapides inside a hangar at Ghaleh Morghi. While it is known that all three Iranian Rapides were painted in overall black upon delivery, the white top of the aircraft in the photo, raises the question if more than the three announced Rapides might have been delivered to Iran. (Babak Taghvaee)

Hawker Hurricane Mk.I L2079 undergoing heavy maintenance inside a Ghaleh Morghi hangar. (Captain Jahangir Salem)

Despite the fact that the Hurricane Mk.I was not equipped with a tropical filter, it performed satisfactory in Iran's high and hot environments. As a result, said aircraft was purchased for the Iranian air force. It received serial 2-51 and was used for pilot training.

With the Shah's eagerness to modernise his military and replace his air force's obsolete biplanes with modern monoplanes, the planned six-month trial period was shortened to two months and an order for 30 Hurricane Mk.Is with Merlin-III engines and 24 Spitfire Mk.Is was placed on 21 December 1939 with the Hawker and Supermarine companies, respectively. However, with the outbreak of the Second World War earlier in September 1939, the British Air Ministry agreed to release only 16 Hurricanes from RAF inventory, which were to be dispatched between March and September 1940. The delivery was further delayed due to problems with the development of the tropical air filter for the Hurricane which was a necessity for the sandy environments of North African and the Middle East. With Great Britain's deeper involvement in the war, the Iranian Hurricane and Spitfire contract was eventually cancelled, and no other British fighter aircraft was delivered to Iran before the Anglo-Soviet Invasion.[8]

AIRSPEED AS.10 OXFORD

In March 1939, three ex-RAF Airspeed AS.10 Oxford Mk.Is (P1984, P1993 and P2002 built in Portsmouth, UK) were delivered to Iran from the RAF East Command in India. They were shipped in crates aboard an Australian merchant ship from Calcutta, India, to the port of Khoramshahr. There, they were transported to Ahvaz by road. After assembly by RAF maintenance crew, all three were test flown by Airspeed test pilot Brian Field and flown to Dowshan Tappeh airbase. In Iranian service they received serials 801, 802 and 803 respectively.

The three-seat Oxford's service in Iranian military was significant for four reasons. Not only was the Oxford the first twin-engine military aircraft in Iranian service, it was also the first Iranian aircraft with retractable landing gear fitted with brakes. Finally, it was the last aircraft to enter IIAF service before the Second World War broke out and the last aircraft to join the Iranian air force during Reza Shah's rule.

IIAF Oxfords wore the standard RAF transport command camouflage, which consisted of dark green and brown camouflage with yellow undersides, until the end of their service. While the primary role of the dual-control Oxford in the IIAF service was a multi-engine trainer, they were also used to train navigators, bombardiers and air gunners until the arrival of the Avro Ansons in 1946. The three Oxfords were maintained and services by the RAF personnel at the Shahbaz State Aircraft Factory.

A bombardier's station with a vertically aimed bombsight was located in the glazed nose compartment, with the navigator/radio operator station right behind it. An electrically powered, revolving dorsal gun turret, armed with a single-barrel Armstrong-Whitworth 7.7mm (0.303 in) Vickers 'K' gas-operated machine gun was located mid-way atop the main cabin. The turret could be removed, if required. For training of bombardiers, there was a provision to carry sixteen 11.5lb (5.2kg) practice bombs externally. Each aircraft was equipped with night flying capabilities. The aircraft was also fitted with a fixed-focal lens reconnaissance camera, as well as navigation and wireless radio equipment.

One of three Iranian Airspeed AS.10 Oxfords, 802, during deployment to Robat-e-Karim for reconnaissance missions in 1940. Note the absence of the machine gun in the turret. (L'Avion 8-1956)

In May 1939, the three Oxfords formed the 5th Light Bomber Squadron at Dowshan Tappeh air base, however, the need for a communication aircraft saw them utilised more as transport/liaison aircraft rather than as a bomber. In that role, they transported military personnel and cargo between the air bases during the internal conflict of the late 1930s.

In a military operation at Jahrom and Susangerd in July 1939, Oxford '802' evacuated no fewer than 10 badly injured soldiers from the scene while under enemy fire and at overloaded capacity. For use as a military transport, the aircraft's machine gun turret, floor camera and bombardier's station had been removed to provide space and added payload capacity to carry maximum number of soldiers in the main cabin.

Oxford '801' was used as a commercial transport, albeit with a military crew. This aircraft was later equipped with a VIP interior for the personal use of Reza Shah. However, the Shah preferred travelling by train over flying and never flew in this or in fact in any other aircraft.

Due to lack of landing strips throughout the country to deploy ground troops by transport aircraft, an order to establish an airborne division within the Army was issued and Army Colonel M. Lavayee was sent to France for parachute training.

After the completion of his training and return to Iran, Colonel Lavayee was tasked to determine if the Airspeed Oxford, the only transport aircraft in IIAF service, was suitable for parachute jumping. On 17 December 1939, he performed the first parachute jumping in Iran from Oxford '803' while the aircraft was piloted by Lieutenant Hassan Toofanian (later General and Deputy Minister of War). With its side door removed, Colonel Lavayee jumped from an altitude of 1,500 metres over Dowshan Tappeh airbase, using two non-standard parachutes, normally used by pilots, to bail out of their aircraft in case of an emergency.

Army Colonel M. Lavayee, the first Iranian paratrooper, was responsible for the establishment of the first Airborne Division of the Iranian Army. (History of Iran)

Within less than a month he established a training centre for parachute jumping and within less than a year the first Airborne Division of the Iranian Army was formed. When all three Oxfords were assigned to the 1st Army Airborne Division, their gun turrets, bombing stations and the floor cameras were removed to allow the carrying of between five and seven fully equipped paratroopers.

The aircraft side doors were also permanently removed. However, the small door was located close and level with the horizontal stabilisers and thus posed a major risk for the exiting paratroopers to be struck by the aircraft. Thus anyone who jumped from the aircraft door was required to make a steep downwards exit from the aircraft.

No records are available to indicate if any of the Oxfords were actually used for paradropping in a combat operation.[9] Later in 1946, Oxford '801' was equipped with Zenith-503.C2 cartographic camera and used for mapping the railroad extension routes in the province of Kurdistan. During one such mission at the Zagros Mountain range, '801' crashed into the mountain due to a wrong setting of its altimeter, killing the entire crew of four onboard.

In another accident, Oxford '803' was badly damaged during a hard landing at Birjand on 2 April 1947. It was repaired, but was involved in another accident at Rezaiyeh airport, on 18 September 1951, when its right wing clipped a military fuel truck. This caused the aircraft's wing to be partially separated from the fuselage engulfing the right engine in fire, which burned down half of the fuselage. Its crew of three escaped with minor injuries but the aircraft was written off and scrapped later. The ultimate fate of '802' remains unknown to this date.

IIAF ORGANISATION IN THE 1930s

In 1934, the structure of the Persian air power was based on the original four regiments. With the delivery of more aircraft and increased number of personnel, the first composite wing under command of Colonel Ahmad Khosravani was established in June 1934 at Ghaleh Morghi airfield. Considered a part of the composite wing was a maintenance department under the command of Colonel Seyed Mohammad Mohana, with a technical school, three repair hangars, carpentry, sheet metal and fabric cutting workshops at the south end of Ghaleh Morghi. However, all maintenance facilities were transferred to Dowshan Tappeh airfield, east of Tehran, in 1935.

With the arrival of 20 additional DH.82 and DH.82A Tiger Moths (c/n 3290-3309) in January and February 1936, followed by another 10 in May (c/n 3464-3473), training squadrons were expanded in all four regiments. By 1 October 1936, the Iranian air force had about 168 aircraft on hand as reported in Table 14. As per another IIAF document, a partial order of battle on 20 November 1939 was as shown in Table 15.

Table 13: Structure of IIAF combat units in 1934

1st Regiment – Tehran – Established 1934				
Airfield	**Wing**	**Squadrons**	**Aircraft**	**Qty**
Ghaleh Morghi	1st Composite**	1st Fighter	Hawker Fury	10
		2nd Fighter/Bomber	Hawker Audax	7
		3rd Reconnaissance	DH Tiger Moth	5
	1st Fighter/Bomber Advanced Training	4th Fighter/Bomber Operational trainer	Hawker Audax	8
			N2C-1 Fledgling	1
Dowshan Tappeh	2nd Composite**	1st Training	DH Tiger Moth	5
		2nd Training	DH Tiger Moth	5
	Basic training	3rd Training	Hawker Audax* Polikarpov U-1	2 3
		4th Bomber/ Reconnaissance	Polikarpov R-5	9
		5th Reconnaissance	Tiger Moth	4
*Dual-control, Hornet-powered **The two composite wings were active until August 1941, when they moved to Isfahan following the invasion of the Allied forces and were soon disbanded.				
2nd Regiment – Tabriz – Established 1934				
Tabriz	2nd Fighter	2nd Fighter	Hawker Audax	12
		4th Training	DH Tiger Moth	6
			Polikarpov R-1	8
3rd Regiment – Mashhad – Established 1935				
Mashhad	3rd Fighter	3rd Fighter	Hawker Audax	3
		5th Training	Hawker Fury	2
			DH Tiger Moth	2
4th Regiment – Ahvaz – Established 1935				
Ahvaz	4th Fighter	4th Fighter	Hawker Audax	3
			Polikarpov R-1	9
		6th Training	DH Tiger Moth	2

Table 14: IIAF aircraft on charge on 1 October 1936

Number	**Type**	**Notes**
68	Tiger Moth	18 with Gipsy-III and 50 with Gipsy Major engines
21	Audax	Hornet engines
18	Audax	Pegasus engines
16	Hawker Fury	Mercury engines
10	Polikarpov R-5	M-17 engines
2	Junkers W 33	L-5 engines
11	Polikarpov R-1	M-5 engines (5 aircraft were without engines)
1	Curtiss Fledgling	Wright J-5 (220hp)
3	Polikarpov U-1	Gnome Monosoupape engine

Table 15: Partial IIAF order of battle on 20 November 1939

1st Regiment, Tehran **Commander: Colonel Ahmad Khosravani, until 1936, then Colonel Khalil Marjan**			
Units	Aircraft	Available	Under maintenance
Tehran (Ghaleh Morghi / Dowshan Tappeh)	Hind	33	n/a
	Fury	14	
	Audax	25 +1*	
	Tiger Moth	15	
	Hurricane Mk.IC	1	
	Polikarpov R-5	6	
Mehrabad Flying School	Tiger Moth	51	7
	Hind (dual-control)	2	0
	Audax**	9	10
	Fury	3	7
* target towing aircraft ** 3 were dual-control aircraft			

6

THE SECOND WORLD WAR

CURTISS H-75 HAWK

After the refusal of Great Britain to deliver the requested 30 Hurricanes and 24 Spitfires, Iran turned to the United States. In November 1939, an IIAF delegation consisting of Lieutenant Colonel Khosravani, Major Shalchi and Captain Afghami, left for the USA. At the same time, the premier American aircraft manufacturer of the 1930s and 40s, the Curtiss Airplane Company, had gained permission from the US government to export a version of its US Army P-36A fighter. Without any hesitation, the visiting Iranian team ordered 10 model H75A-9s.

This model was the last in the H75A retractable gear Curtiss Hawk line, powered by a 1,200hp Wright R-1820-G205A Cyclone radial engine at 2,500rpm and 44 inches of manifold pressure for take-off, and 1,100hp at 2,500rpm at 5,100 feet and 40 inches of manifold pressure. There was a provision for four Colt 7.92mm (0.30) wing-mounted machine guns, however, those were not installed on Iranian machines upon delivery. The H-75 had a simple ring-and-bead gun sight, an RCA AVT-12B radio transmitter, as well as an AVR-7G receiver.

The 10 aircraft under sales order No.202 were accepted in the United States between 9 March and 4 April 1941. These were Curtiss construction number 15252–15261, and the cost for Iran was set at $37,689 per aircraft. These aircraft received Iranian serials 252–261 (the last three digits of their msn).

The first aircraft, 252, used to test the minor modifications required for the Iranian operational environment, was delivered in June by Curtiss test pilot Sam Irwin, who also tested the aircraft in Iranian weather conditions. The other nine arrived at the port of Khoramshahr in crates on 18 August 1941.

However, before they could be assembled, they were captured by British forces who had entered Iran on 25 August 1941, along with Soviet forces, during the Allied occupation of Iran. The captured crates were rerouted to India without being unpacked. Upon arrival in India they were assembled by the newly established Hindustan Aircraft Industry (HAL) and pressed into RAF Far East Command as Mohawk Mk.IVs. They received RAF serials LA157–LA165 and served with 'A' flight, No. 1 Operational Training Unit (OTU-India) and later No.151 (Fighter) OTU at Risalpur.

The fuselage of a brand-new Curtiss H75A-9 Hawk with the Imperial crown and serial 257 already painted in Farsi numerals at Curtiss Aircraft factory. (Museum of Flight)

One of the Persian Curtiss H75A-9s being test flown near Buffalo, NY, in early 1941. The yellow cowl is noteworthy and the blue cast to some of the metal surfaces was a special coating applied to protect the aluminium during manufacture. The Persian Hawks were armed with two 0.50 machine guns mounted in the engine cowl synchronised to fire through the propeller, and four 0.30 machine guns mounted in the wings (installed after delivery),v just outside of the propeller arc. (Museum of Flight)

The first Hawk that was delivered to the IIAF remained in Iran and was issued RAF serial LA166. While it is reported that the sole assembled H75 remained in Iranian air force service as an operational trainer based at Mehrabad Training school until 1951, it is also reported that it was flown to Iraq by an American pilot and pressed into RAF service as HK823. The definite final fate of H75 252 remains unknown to this day. While the Hawk 75 never became operational as a type in IIAF service, it marked the first US-built aircraft ordered for the Iranian air force. It also marked the end of three decades of British dominance in Iranian military affairs.

GERMANS IN IRAN

From the beginning of the Pahlavi dynasty in 1925, Persia (Iran after 1935), had established close ties with Germany. The start of Junkers' transportation service in 1924 had already paved the way for the involvement of Germany in Persian affairs.

The first king of Pahlavi, Reza Shah, was openly pro-German, partially because of his passion for German discipline and punctuality, but mostly due to his dislike of the British and mistrust of the Soviets as foreign powers with an Imperialistic history in the region. As a result, he was determined to minimise the influence of the latter two in Iranian internal affairs. The Germans on the other hand greatly emphasised the two countries' common interests and racial ties as 'pure Aryans'.

Reza Shah turned to Germany for assistance to carry out his ambitious economical, industrial and social reform programmes. Germany was involved in building and improving the industrial infrastructure in Persia with ports, roads, air transport network, railroads, bridges, tunnels, factories, hospitals and schools.

To stay away from hostilities and to concentrate on modernisation plans, Iran immediately declared its neutrality when the Second World War broke out in September 1939. In 1941, however, Iran was hosting about a thousand German residents, far fewer than the 2,000 to 7,000 claimed by the Allies. Little more than 300 of them were German officials and their families, including a few Gestapo operatives, military attachés and intelligence officers.

The rest of the German residents were contractors working for the Iranian government. Iran's vulnerability to invasion increased considerably once London and Moscow became allies against Hitler. This was because the Allies needed to open supply corridors to the Soviet Union as an alternative to the hazardous Arctic routes. In addition, the Allies sought to protect oil installations in Iran and Baku from German attack.

This, in turn, required the Allies to uproot German influence in Iran and eliminate the potential German threat to their interests. At every opportunity, the Allies expressed their concern that Iran, with its pro-German leader, might become a member of the Axis in the Middle East for the expansion plans of the Third Reich. In case of a German invasion of Iran, the vast oilfields of Khuzestan and Khorasan provinces, along with the Abadan refinery (the largest in the world at the time, owned and operated by the AIOC),[1] could fall in the hands of Nazi Germany and fuel its war machine.

On the other hand, the speedy advance of the *Wehrmacht* (German Armed Forces) on the Eastern Front caused concern as during the summer of 1941 it seemed unstoppable. It had crushed the Red Army in several battles and was marching towards the oil-rich Caucasus. Thus, it was crucial for the British to provide Lend-Lease military supplies to the Soviet Union as they were desperately needed.

With the increasing German U-boat threat and ice conditions in the Arctic eight months a year, sending the military convoys to the port of Arkhangelsk and Murmansk was becoming extremely dangerous. Securing the Iranian route and its railway network was seen as an easier and safer alternative route to supply military equipment to the Soviet Union and with merchant losses to U-boats mounting, the route through Iran was becoming increasingly attractive.

In 1941, Britain and the Soviet Union issued multiple diplomatic ultimatums to the Iranian government on 19 and 25 July, and again on 5 and 17 August demanding the expulsion of all Axis nationals as quickly as possible, citing them to be spies and Gestapo agents operating undercover as businessmen. But Reza Shah was not ready to expel any Germans, thus, no response was issued by the Iranian government to the Allied demands. As a result, British and Soviet forces invaded Iran in a coordinated military operation, codenamed Operation Countenance, on 25 August 1941.

THE ALLIED INVASION

British forces entered Iran from the west and south-west, while the Soviets invaded from the north-east and north-west. As the Allied forces crossed Iranian borders, their respective ambassadors in Tehran demanded that Iran accept British and Soviet protection of oil supplies.

The British forces, under the command of Lieutenant General Edward Quinan, were made up of the 8th and 10th Indian Infantry Divisions, the 2nd Indian Armoured Brigade, the 4th British Cavalry Brigade, and the 21st Indian Infantry Brigade.

The 10th Division entered Iran from two points: the first one from Qasr-e-Shirin advancing through the Paitak pass; the second from Naft-e-Shah, which advanced to Shahabad. After these joined up, the 10th Division moved to Kermanshah, Hamadan and Qum. The 8th Division entered from Basra, capturing Abadan, Khoramshahr,

Dressed in full uniform, typical of the Third Reich, German air force, army and navy attachés to Iran watch a military parade of the Iranian army from their VIP stand at the Jalalieh stadium, Tehran, 1939. (WW2 Iran Pictorial)

and moving north to Ahvaz, Masjed-Soleyman, and Dezful, while securing the Abadan refinery and all oilfields. The Iranian armoured formations were defeated after offering a light resistance. The British and Soviet ground forces met each other in Qazvin, some 100km west of Tehran and moved towards the capital city.

Despite the fact that the main operation was carried out by Allied ground forces, British and Soviet air forces participated in the invasion as well and were successful in suppressing scattered Iranian resistance in the south-western provinces of Khuzestan, Kermanshah; north-eastern province of Khorasan and north-western provinces of East and West Azerbaijan. Obviously, the Iranian air force, with its limited number of obsolete biplanes and inexperienced pilots, was not much of a match for the larger and more modern British Royal Air Force and the Soviet Air Force.

On the morning of 25 August 1941, the IIAF under the command of Brigadier General Ahmad Khosravani, and Colonel Mahmoud Khosravani as chief-of-Staff, had aircraft in its inventory as shown in Table 16, and was organised into four regiments as shown in Table 17.

Table 16: IIAF aircraft inventory on 25 August 1941

Quantity	Type	Notes
49	Hawker Audax	Out of 56 delivered plus 10 built by the Shahbaz State Factory
15	Hawker Fury Mk.I/II	Out of 24 delivered
28	Hawker Hind	Out of 35 delivered plus 20 built by Shahbaz
2	Dragon Rapide	
1	Curtiss Fledgling	
1	RWD-13	
3	Airspeed Oxford Mk.I	
1	Hawker Hurricane Mk.I	(without tropical filters and guns)
1	Praga E.114	
82	Tiger Moths	Out of 99 delivered plus 10 built by Shahbaz
5	Polikarpov R-5	Out of 10 delivered

Table 17: Organisation of the IIAF on 25 August 1941

1st Regiment, Tehran Ghaleh Morghi, Tehran Dowshan Tappeh, Mehrabad			
Units	**Aircraft**	**Available**	**Under maintenance**
2 fighter-bomber squadrons at Tehran Ghaleh Morghi	Audax	17	3
	Fury	4	1
1 fighter-recce squadron at Tehran Ghaleh Morghi	Audax	4	0
	Hind*	6	1**
	Tiger Moth	14	1**
1 transport-utility squadron at Tehran Ghaleh Morghi	Dragon Rapide	2	0
	Oxford Mk.I	3	0
	E.114	1	0
	RWD-13	1	0
1 training-observation squadron at Tehran Dowshan Tappeh	Tiger Moth	13	3***
	Hind (dual-control)	2	0
	Hurricane Mk.I	1	0
	Fledgling	1	0
Training School at Mehrabad	Tiger Moth	17	00
	Hind (dual-control)	2	0
48 pilots, 11 observers and 31 mechanics on duty in the entire regiment. * Four Hinds were equipped with Zeiss-Humber 23-44 cameras. ** No engine. *** One Tiger Moth had no engine			
2nd Regiment, Tabriz (Colonel Gholamhossein Sheibani)			
2 fighter-bomber squadrons at Tabriz	Audax	13	1*
	Fury	3	1**
1 fighter-bomber squadron at Tabriz	Hind	4	0
1 training-observation squadron at Tabriz	Tiger Moth	14	2*
	R-5	3	0
28 pilots, 8 observers and 18 mechanics on duty. * No engine(s). ** Damaged in hard landing			
3rd Regiment, Masshad (Major Darab Jahansuz)			
2 fighter-bomber squadrons at Masshad	Audax	7	0
	Fury	4	0
	Hind	8	0
1 light bomber-recce squadron at Masshad	Tiger Moth	11	1
1 training-observation squadron at Masshad	Tiger Moth	3	0
	R-5	2	0
35 pilots, 11 observers and 12 mechanics on duty.			
4th Regiment, Ahvaz (Major Hedayat Gilanshah)			
2 fighter-bomber squadrons at Ahvaz	Audax	7	2
	Fury	2	0
	Hind	5	0
	Tiger Moth	8	2
11 pilots, 6 observers and 9 mechanics on duty			

AIR OPERATIONS DURING OPERATION COUNTENANCE

The first intrusion of the Royal Air Force into Iranian airspace on the morning of 25 August was made by six Bristol Blenheim Mk.Is from No. 11 Squadron based at Habbaniya, Iraq, entering from the Ghasre-Shirin area.[2] Despite being armed with bombs, no attack was carried out against any Iranian target. Instead, they dropped leaflets written in Farsi, over Abadan, Khoramshahr, Khanighin, Haftkel, Masjid-Suleyman and Ahvaz, explaining the reason of the invasion and the good intentions of Allies in protecting the Iranian people, industries and oilfields from attacks by Nazi Germany.

The next morning, three RAF Westland Wapities entered Iran and bombed Iranian convoys along the Abadan-Ahvaz road and military depots. On 26 August, a Hurricane from No. 261 Squadron shot down an Iranian Audax over the Haftkel oilfields. The same aircraft also attacked and shot down one of its own by mistake, a Vincent from No. 244 Squadron. On the morning of 27 August, a single Vickers Wellesley Mk.I of No. 14 Squadron bombed a maintenance hangar at Abadan airport during which 1st Sergeant Jamshid Sahmi, a mechanic working in the hangar, was killed and three aircraft of unknown types were destroyed.

In the afternoon, three Vickers Vincents of No. 11 Squadron, based at Shaibah in Iraq, bombed and strafed Iranian convoys attempting to build up a defensive force to resist the invading armies, some 15 miles south of the city of Andimeshk.

On 28 August, No. 84 Squadron Blenheims attacked Ahvaz airport and shot down Fury 219, flown by 1st Lieutenant Ahmad Ghaem-Maghami, who was attempting to take-off. Other RAF units who faced limited Iranian resistance were No. 84 Squadron with Bristol Blenheim Mk.IVs, No 261 Squadron with Hawker Hurricanes and Gloster Gladiators, No. 244 Squadron with Vickers Vincents and No. 31 Squadron, A Flight, with six Vickers Valentia transports.

The RAF reported to have destroyed six Iranian aircraft by strafing, four during dogfights, one attempting to take-off and three others in a hangar. As mentioned before, the British forces also captured the nine Curtiss H75A-9 still in crates at the port of Khoramshahr. Also, the Shahbaz State Aircraft Factory ceased production and RAF No. 138 Maintenance and Repair Unit were housed at the premises.

In the north, the Soviet forces under the command of General Dmitri Timofeyevich Kozlov were comprised of the 44th and 47th Armies from the Trans-Caucasian Military District, and the 53rd Detachment from the Independent Central Asian Army. Air units included the 36th and 265th IAP (Fighter Air Regiments) flying Polikarpov I-16 fighters. Due to the small size and antiquated state of the Iranian air force, the Soviets mostly utilised older aircraft. However, at least three more modern Yak-1s were seen at Tabriz airport.

The 44th Army entered Iran with two brigades. The western brigade from Pole-Dasht advanced and captured Maku, Khoy and Rezaiyeh. The eastern brigade entered from Julfa and captured Marand and Tabriz, and moved south in two directions towards Zanjan and Qazvin and to Miandoab and Senneh. The 47th Army entered from Astara, advanced to and captured Ardabil and Rasht and joined the 44th Army in Qazvin. The 53rd Army entered Iran from three points into the eastern province of Khorasan and captured

RAF Westland Wapities entered Iranian airspace from Ghasre-Shirin and bombed Iranian convoys along the Abadan-Ahvaz road and at the Aghajari military depot. (Air Enthusiast)

Royal Air Force Gloster Gladiators at Shaibah air base, Iraq, from where they launched attacks on Iranian targets in Khuzestan during the 1941 invasion of Iran. (Air Power Illustrated)

One of three Vickers Wellesley Mk.Is of No. 14 Squadron, which bombed a maintenance hangar at Abadan airport and a storage depot at the port of Khoramshahr. (Persian Times)

A Soviet Air Force I-16 from 36th Fighter Regiment flying over Tabriz Blue Mosque. (Pravda)

Personal note on the photo identifies this Soviet Air Force 36th Fighter Regiment Yak-1 fighter to be located at Tabriz, August 1941. (Russian Heritage Collection)

Gorgan, Bojnurd, Quchan, Gonbad-e-Qabus, and Mashhad. In addition, commandos of the Soviet Caspian fleet landed and secured the ports of Astara and Anzali.

According to Iranian reports, Tabriz, Ardabil, Rezaiyeh, Rasht, Mashhad, and Ghochan were attacked by Soviet bombers, but Soviet records mention only reconnaissance and leaflet dropping sorties. The 2nd Regiment based at Tabriz was only able to conduct a few reconnaissance sorties, during which they were chased by Soviet Yaks. The Iranian air defence was able to shoot down one I-16 fighter some 18 miles northwest of Maraghe.

On the early morning of 26 August, Colonel Sheibani, the commander of the 2nd Regiment at Tabriz received an order from Tehran headquarters to move all aircraft to Zanjan. Due to shortage of pilots and observers, only eight Hawker Audaxes and six Hawker Hinds could be saved. All aircraft were loaded up with any weapon or spare part possible, from machine guns and ammunition to fuel pumps and tires.

They started to take-off at around 3am. Despite the fact that most of the pilots had no experience in night flying and navigation, 12 aircraft reached Zanjan. The first aircraft to land was Colonel Sheibani's Audax. Two aircraft made an emergency landing on Talesh Mountain. Both aircraft were written off, but the crew sustained only minor injuries and were able to walk to the nearby village and get rescued by the locals. All 12 aircraft flew to Tehran the following day and landed at Dowshan Tappeh airbase. When Tabriz was taken on 28 August the Soviets captured some of the remaining Audax and Hind aircraft. They were sent to a Soviet fighter wing in Armenia and some ended up with the VVS.

The situation was not any better on the eastern front. The Soviet 53rd Army air units had seven Ilyushin Il-2s and four Petlyakov Pe-2 twin-engine reconnaissance bombers, which bombed Mashhad airport and destroyed most of the 3rd Regiment's aircraft.

The commander of the 3rd Regiment, Major Darab Jahansuz, ordered all remaining aircraft to retreat to Torogh airport, a small airfield with a dirt landing strip and a single small hangar. Since the

Russian 265th Fighter Regiment I-16 pilots are reviewing the maps at a landing field near Maku, east Azerbaijan province. (Russian Heritage Collection)

A Soviet 53rd Army Air Unit Ilyushin Il-2 flying over the city of Mashhad with its famous Goharshad Mosque. Their surprise attack on Mashhad airport destroyed a large portion of the 3rd Regiment's aircraft on the ground. (Russian Heritage Collection)

A Russian Petlyakov Pe-2 bomber lands on a dirt strip near Quchan, Iran. They participated in bombing Iranian army barracks at Mashhad, Ghuchan and Nishapur. (Russian Heritage Collection)

airfield was not suitable and safe for a long stay, the squadron was further moved back to Sabzevar airport.

One Hawker Hind, piloted by Captain Reza Falahi, made an emergency landing near Kashmer due to bad weather. Major Jahansuz and his mechanic carried fuel and oil to the landing site and after servicing Captain Falahi's aircraft, the mechanic left for Sabzevar by car, and Major Jahansuz and Captain Falahi took off for Sabzevar, but their aircraft crashed 65 miles east of Sabzevar due to engine failure, killing both crew members.

The 4th Regiment at Ahvaz was on alert following the British military operation in Iraq a few months earlier. However, being unaware of Allied landing at the Iranian ports, the 4th Regiment was caught by surprise. In the early morning of 25 August, three RAF Hurricanes strafed Ahvaz airfield killing mechanics 2nd Sergeant Seyyed Ali Toluee and 1st Sergeant Abbas Farzanefar. By noon, four Gloster Gladiators had bombed the Abadan-Ahvaz road, preventing the retreating Iranian tanks from moving north.

On 27 August, Soviet paratroopers landed at Ghaleh Morghi while Mehrabad airfield was captured by British forces. The occupation of Iran resulted in the opening of the 'Persian Corridor'. Dubbed by the Allies as 'The Bridge to Victory', the Trans-Iranian route allowed Lend-Lease military supplies to reach the Soviet Union from ports on the Persian Gulf.

THE PERSIAN CORRIDOR

On 11 March 1941, a year and half after the outbreak of the Second World War in Europe in September 1939 and nine months before the entry of the United States into the war in December 1941, President Roosevelt signed the Lend-Lease Bill into law which allowed the US to give military aid and supplies to the Allies without them having to pay for it first. Used equipment would be returned once the war was over.

Under this arrangement the US supplied military equipment to Great Britain, the Soviet Union, Free France, Republic of China, and other Allied nations between March 1941 and August 1945. A total of $50.1 billion ($658 billion today) worth of supplies, ranging from aircraft, tanks, artillery, and trucks, to ammunition, medical supplies, tents, even canned foods were delivered to Allied nations. A large part of this aid went to the Soviet Union, due to the fact that at one point the *Wehrmacht* was only 42 miles from Moscow and was moving south toward the oil-rich Caucasus.

The Lend-Lease Program was divided into multiple protocols. Each protocol, named after the capital of an allied country, clearly specified the items to be delivered and its completion timetable. The slogan of the Lend-Lease was 'skill, spirit and supply are the essentials for the victory'. However, without the third, the first two could not prevail.

Thus, the most challenging issue for the Lend-Lease Program to succeed was the delivery of materials. Even before the United States entered the war on the Allied side in December 1941, the first 'Moscow' protocol was signed on 1 October 1941. It obligated the United States to supply the Soviets with a large number of aircraft. It posed the formidable question of how to deliver these to the embattled country.

Through the four Lend-Lease routes over 17.5 million long tons of supplies were carried from the Western Hemisphere to Soviet destinations. Tanks were loaded in ships and aircraft were delivered by either direct flights or disassembled and shipped in 6,577 crates, carried by 2,803 ships.

The Americans hoped that aircraft could be primarily flown via Alaska across Siberia to Soviet collection points convenient to the battle areas in the USSR. After long delays they learned that the Soviets, suspecting the Americans wished flight route information for strategic reasons, would refuse to approve any arrangement for delivery which involved flight by American pilots across Soviet territory. As a result, American aircraft were flown to Fairbanks, Alaska, where they were taken onward by Soviet pilots.

For the second route, the Soviets proposed delivery via ship to the ports of Arkhangel and Murmansk through the Arctic Ocean. However, the increasing threat of German U-boats in the area, which had already sunk 186 Allied merchant ships, plus severe icing conditions of the Arctic made the route slow and dangerous.

As a third option, the Soviet Union offered to have their own shipping companies handle the supplies from the West Coast of the United States and Canada to the port of Vladivostok in the Far East, since the Soviet Union was not at war with Japan until August 1945, but that route required a long overland journey from that most eastern ports of Russia to their western front using the Trans-Siberian railroad.

Finally, Allied forces concluded that Persia's geographical position would offer the safest and most accessible route to get Lend-Lease supplies to the Soviets. The proposed Persian Corridor would join Soviet territory to the warm waters of the Persian Gulf and the Arabian Sea across the mountains and deserts of Iran.

Emblem of the Persian Gulf Command. (Iranian markings database)

The Persian Corridor became part of the US Army Military Mission Iran, part of the US Army Corps of Engineers in September 1941. It was reassigned to the 'Persian Gulf Service Command', which was officially created in August 1942. In December 1943 it became the 'Persian Gulf Command'.

The sea voyage from New York to the Persian Gulf would normally take 70–75 days by circling the African continent around the Cape of Hope in South Africa. However, after the Allied forces captured Crete and Sicily in 1943 and cleared the Axis naval forces from the Mediterranean, the time to get to the Persian Gulf through the Suez Canal was shortened to 40–42 days.

The ports of Bandar Khoramshahr, Bandar Shahpur and Bandar Boushehr,[3] were operated by US troops and served for the entry of Lend-Lease supplies en route to the USSR. However, their docking spaces were often insufficient to accommodate all ships waiting to be unloaded. Only one dock in each terminus could handle large ships. On the other hand, the Trans-Iranian Railway lacked capacity. The railway from the port of Bandar Shahpur to Tehran and then to the Soviet Union was light rail through mountains. As a result, as late as 1944, supplies ordered and delivered in 1942 were still waiting for transit to the Soviet Union.

US M4 Sherman tanks destined for Russia being transported by Trans Iranian Railways. No fewer than 8,015 tanks, 4,509 artillery guns and 15,308 jeeps were transported by train to the border city of Julfa, in addition to 17,435 military trucks driven by road to the collection points at the Armenian border. (US Army Archive)

The aerial view of enormous aircraft assembly facilities at Abadan. The Douglas Aircraft Company and the US Army turned the former Anglo-Iranian Oil Company's small airfield into one of the largest military facilities outside the United States. (WW2 Stats)

After the US entered the war, it took on a more active role and increased the corridor's tonnage to the second largest among all the supply routes to the USSR. Basically 50% of the total Lend-Lease tonnage shipped to the USSR was transported through the Persian Corridor. However, this was not the only Allied contribution via the Persian Corridor.

About 7,900,000 long tons (8,000,000 metric tons) of shipboard cargo from Allied sources unloaded in the corridor was bound for the USSR. This tonnage figure does not include transfers of warplanes via Persia. Another 4,159,117 long tons (4,225,858 metric tons) of supplies that were also unloaded at the three Iranian ports was sent to the British forces in Iraq, Palestine and Egypt under the Middle East Command, but a significant portion was allocated for development of new roads, bridges, airfields and logistics facilities in Iran and supporting its economy.

AIRCRAFT ASSEMBLY IN IRAN

The Douglas Aircraft Company had been selected in October 1941 to manage and operate the Persian Corridor in cooperation with the US Army and the British Middle East Command. It was also ordered to establish an aircraft assembly plant at Abadan, in a large open area three miles north of the Anglo-Iranian Oil Company refinery. For this purpose, a gravel strip was flattened for test flying of assembled aircraft. The aircraft assembly operation was called Project Cedar (Civilian Emergency Defense Aid to Russia).

On 17 May, 356 Douglas employees arrived in Abadan. These, along with nine Army Air Corps officers and 42 enlisted men and supported by over 1,400 native workers, started the erection of the aircraft assembly plant on 20 May. The first ship that arrived in Abadan delivered two prefabricated hangars, 14 warehouses, 120 Quonset huts, and 10 Dimaxion circular huts ready for quick erection.

Previously, the AIOC had constructed an airfield for its own use at the same location with three hangars, eight brick offices and shop buildings, 36 Indian huts and one 5,500ft-long paved runway which was later extended to 6,500ft, and a hard-surface apron in front of Hangars 1 and 2.

Aside from the assembly buildings and hangars, major construction work started on power supply, connecting roads, storage, warehouse, living quarters, hospital, repair depot, telephone-radios, water supply and sewage system. The US Army constructed additional roads, extended rail tracks to allow trains to pass each other without waiting, built additional port docks and brought in diesel locomotives and rolling stock in large numbers from the United States.

Douglas A-20 Boston bombers under assembly in Hangar-2. 1,269 A-20B/G/H, 151 Douglas DB-7, and 124 North American B-25C/C1 aircraft were assembled at Abadan and delivered to the Soviet Union. (US Army)

The Douglas Aircraft assembly plant at Abadan, under contract of the US Army Air Corps, assembled 1,025 aircraft (an average of 64 aircraft per month) in the first 16 months of its operation for delivery to the Soviet Union by Soviet pilots. Of the 14,834 American aircraft made available to the Soviet Union under lend-lease, 4,874 were delivered via the Persian Corridor, of which 995 were flown in and 3,879 were shipped in crates. Upon arrival these aircraft required assembly, refit and test flights.

After the test flight, the aircraft either flew directly to collection points in Soviet Armenia or Azerbaijan or went through a final check point at Tehran's Dowshan Tappeh airfield, which was jointly occupied by the US and Soviet forces at the time.

The construction cost of Project Cedar was $7,259,548.00 (US$159 million today), and the cost of the work performed under the Douglas contract was US$3,795,735.00. The contract stipulated that the Abadan plant would handle 100 twin-engine light attack bombers (A-20s), 100 single-engine fighters (P-40s), and 12 twin-engine medium bomber (B-25s) every month.

The first Curtiss P-40 Kittyhawk reached the Persian Gulf by ship on 15 November 1942, followed by the first Bell P-39 Airacobra on 8 December. These were followed by over a thousand more during the following year. The flow of airplanes to the Persian Gulf under the Moscow protocol began with the first shipment from New York of four A-20 Boston light twin-engine bombers on 28 November 1941. They were delivered to the Soviets in February. During March only five additional aircraft were delivered, and an accumulated backlog of 33 planes warned that the flow of aircraft was too large to be handled in a timely manner. Although 120 planes were assembled and delivered to the USSR by 31 May, the backlog had reached nearly 200.

To add to the workload of the aircraft assembly plant in Abadan, on 2 February crews started to modify the first A-20 Boston bombers, originally built to RAF specifications, to Soviet specifications. Most of the modifications were made to the aircraft's radios and armament. However, because of the critical need for aircraft in North Africa where the Allies were fighting in the desert west of Cairo, 40 A-20s consigned to the USSR were released on 11 July and flown to Egypt.

Before Pearl Harbor, American pilots flew planes from the Persian Gulf to the collection points, however, once the US declared war on the Axis, the shortage of American pilots available for transport duties led to agreement with the Soviets to pick up the aircraft themselves.

On 2 May 1942, B-25 assembly was moved from Shaibah in Iraq to Tehran, where in January 1943 the RAF rented the Iranian Aircraft State Factory in Dowshan Tappeh for the assembly of these aircraft.

In order to solve the assembly backlog in Abadan, the Soviets offered to send 148 highly skilled technicians to Iran. Initially, the British Foreign Office would only grant the presence of 10 Soviet technicians at Abadan, but under pressure from the US Army, the British relented in January 1942. An earlier policy to prohibit Soviet aircraft from flying over the British zones in Iran and Iraq was reverted and a larger Soviet presence was permitted at the Abadan facilities.

Soviet mechanics began arriving at Abadan on 22 August and by 8 September all 148 technicians were there to help ease the backlog. However, lack of experience of the Soviets in the assembly of American aircraft and the necessity of Soviet pilots to familiarise themselves with the American planes caused additional delays in deliveries.

Curtiss P-40s at the hangar-1 assembly line. 1,091 P-40E/K-1-CUs, plus 2,030 Bell 39s, 2,406 Bell 63s and 188 P-47D-22-REs were assembled and shipped to Soviet Union. (WW2 stats)

Bell P-39 Airacobras and P-63 Kingcobras were the most numerous American fighters assembled and delivered from the Abadan facilities. (Air Battle.ru)

With the help of the US Army, ports, highways and railroads in Iran were sufficiently ready to handle the amount of increased traffic by the fall of 1942. Under the Lend-Lease agreement, goods became Soviet property at the point of departure from the United States, and therefore Colonel Ivan Obrazkov, chief of the Soviet Air Force personnel in Iran insisted that the planes delivered to them be without any flaws.

Deliveries to the Soviets averaged 182.9 aircraft a month. At its peak in 1943, 2,902 aircraft were delivered. Of these, 197 A-20 and 111 B-25 bombers were flown out, leaving 2,594 aircraft which were assembled after arriving by sea in crates. During the peak, over 40,000 local Iranian workers were employed by the US Army.

July 1944 was the peak of delivered goods, with 282,097 long tons (286,623.8 metric tons) passing through Iran. Counting the 274 A-20 Havoc light bombers which flew across the Atlantic to Abadan, over 5,000 aircraft eventually passed through the Persian Corridor, destined for the Soviet Union. Among the five major types of A-20s delivered, the Soviets received more than two-thirds of all Douglas A-20Bs manufactured, and a significant portion of the G and H models.

For delivery of aircraft through Tehran, Camp Amirabad and the more than 3,000 American troops stationed there played a vital role in support of US Army Air Forces (USAAF) operations at Ghaleh Morghi and Dowshan Tappeh airfields. They provided transport, refuelling, cargo loading, traffic control, maintenance and security at these locations. USAAF C-47s and modified B-24s serving as cargo aircraft flew over 235,000 tons of small arms, ammunition, medical supplies, tents and food to the Soviet border collection points.

Since the northern sector of the Persian Corridor was under Soviet Army command, the Soviets provided pilots for most of the Tehran to Tabriz flights. However, in case an American crew was tasked for the job due to a shortage of pilots, the Soviets required the presence of one of their 'observers' onboard.

THE BRIDGE TO VICTORY

The US Army Military Mission Iran was responsible for the initial construction and extension of over 1,000 miles of all-weather roads, seven steel bridges over the Karun river, 18 high-capacity docks at

The first group of Russian pilots and mechanics disembark from a Russian air force Li-2 at Abadan. Following completion of their training, they flew a large portion of assembled P-39, P-63, P-47, Spitfire, Hurricane, A-20, B-25, B-24, C-47 and T-6 aircraft across the Soviet border. (War memories)

The Soviet Red Star is being painted over the USAAF white star on this C-47. Its former identity, serial number 348130, is still visible under the sprayed overcoat. (History of the Douglas DC3/C-47)

A USAAF Douglas C-47 and a Consolidated B-24 Liberator bomber converted to the transport role, at Dowshan Tappeh, which was under Russian control at the time. A large tonnage of fuel, medical supplies, ammunition, canned food, tents and other essential items were transferred by transport aircraft to the Russian army at the Armenian border. (Iran Zamin archive)

the ports of Khoramshahr and Bandar Shapour, 38 repair depots along the southern sector's roads, four hospitals, and 131 tunnels with a total length of over 37 miles under the Zagros Mountains.

To facilitate transport for overland delivery, two truck assembly plants were established by the General Motors Overseas Corporation at Andimeshk (Plant No.1), and Khoramshahr (Plant No.2). These two locations were selected due to their proximity and access to the Iranian railroad network. A total of 184,286 military trucks, mostly Studebaker US6s (M16A1s), ¾ ton Dodges, Mack Diesels and ½ ton GMCs, were assembled at the two plants between March 1942 and April 1945. In addition, 1,263 trucks destined for the USSR were assembled at Boushehr under contract with the Military Mission. More than 750 experienced Iranian drivers joined the 586 American and 248 Soviet truck drivers to move the convoys that consisted of up to 2,000 cargo-laden trucks at their peak.

However, the largest portion of heavy military hardware, such as tanks, trucks, jeeps, and artillery, was carried by the single-track Iranian State Railways (ISR) Network. The section of rail from Ahvaz to Khoramshahr was built by the British Royal Engineers in 1942. The 3rd Military Railroad Services (MRS) took over the Iranian rail network from the British in January 1943.

Over 1.3 million tons of heavy war material was carried from the Persian Gulf ports to Tehran through 650 miles of single track.

Good old days! Four Russian pilots chat with an American instructor pilot in front of a Spitfire Mk.V at Abadan, wearing a non-standard Persian Gulf Command serial as delivery identification number. (Russian Heritage Collection)

From there the rail continued on to the port of Bandare Shah at the southeastern shore of the Caspian Sea and on to Julfa at the Soviet Armenian border, through Zanjan, Mianeh and Tabriz.

With the 5,000 planes and 200,000 military vehicles delivered, it was officially announced in August 1944 that 50% of the total aid

Convoys of military trucks assembled at Andimeshk took military supplies to the city of Julfa on the Armenian border. The long journey through the challenging trails of the Zagros mountains required special driving skills for convoys which often numbered 2,000 trucks. (Persian Corridor archive)

to the Soviet Union had moved through the Persian Corridor. The mission of the Persian Corridor was declared accomplished by the Chief-of-Staff General of the Army, George C. Marshall, on 1 June 1945. By that time Soviet forces had entered Berlin and the Persian Corridor received its well-deserved "Bridge to Victory" title by Allied nations. If it was not for the Iranian assistance in allowing Allied forces for the unlimited use of its ports, aerodromes, roads and railways, the outcome of the Second World War might have been very different.

The IIAF Avro Anson 705 photographed at Dowshan Tappeh. While the aircraft looks like in an overall dark colour due to poor quality of the photo, it was actually painted in RAF standard brown/green camouflage. (AKTA)

AVRO ANSONS FOR IRAN

On 9 September 1943, Iran declared war on Germany, resulting in Iran joining the Allied camp of belligerents during the Second World War. In response, Great Britain agreed to supply the IIAF with 48 ex-RAF Avro 652A Anson Mk.I light bombers. They were supplied to Iran as a replacement for several orders such as the eight Gloster Gladiators, 20 Bristol Blenheims and 28 Supermarine Spitfires, which never materialised. The Avro Anson delivery was also considered a reward for Iran's support of the war effort that would result in Allied victory.

The Ansons were ordered in four batches and delivered as shown in Table 18.

The Anson was powered by two 350hp Armstrong Siddeley Cheetah IX seven-cylinder, air-cooled radial engines. Its armament consisted of a 0.303in (7.7mm) dorsal turret-mounted Vickers K machine gun, a port side nose-mounted forward-firing 0.303in (7.7mm) machine gun, and 360lbs. (160kg) of bombs under the wings. It was equipped with a bombsight, reconnaissance camera, night navigation compass and dual controls for flight training. These aircraft retained the original RAF brown and green camouflage with medium grey underside.

One more Anson, a Mk.XII, powered by two 420hp Armstrong Siddeley Cheetah XV engines with Rotol constant speed propellers, was fitted with a VIP cabin for personal use of the Shah, who flew the aircraft himself on almost every flight. He also used IIAF Ansons 709 and 719 to fly observation flights during the Azerbaijan and Kurdistan conflicts. Iranian documents identify the Anson serials to range from 160 to 180 and 701 to 727. Unfortunately, their tie-up to RAF serials are unknown.

In July 1944, 15 Iranian pilots and seven technicians were sent to Egypt for training on Ansons. After arrival in Egypt, pilots were sent to a North African RAF base in Ismailia and technicians were sent to Abu-Kheir air base in Alexandria. After completion of their training, they delivered some of the remaining ex-RAF Ansons to Iran. The first batch of refurbished Ansons left Egypt in two groups of three and four, flying over the Sinai Desert, with refuelling stops at Amman, Jordan, and Station-134 at Habbaniya, Iraq, finally landing at Kermanshah, Iran. This was recorded as Iran's longest group delivery flight.

They formed the 1st Bomber Regiment (Wing) at Dowshan Tappeh air base with the 5th and 7th Bomber squadrons, the 12th Navigation Training Squadron and the 4th Reconnaissance Squadron. Being the second twin-engine aircraft in IIAF service, Avro Anson was used as three-to-five seat reconnaissance light bomber, liaison transport, and a conversion trainer for bombing, radio navigation and gunnery.

Table 18: Avro Anson deliveries to Iran

Batch	Ex-RAF Serials
First batch, delivered in May 1944 (7 aircraft)	NK454, NK457, NK510, NK511, NK512, NK516
Second batch, delivered in Nov 1944 (5 aircraft)	AW853, DJ555, NK268, NK271, NK299
Third batch, delivered from Apr to Jun 1945 (35 aircraft)	MG138, MG405, MG685, MG697, MG918, NK185, NK187, NK199, NK200, NK203, NK204, NK227, NK232, NK276, NK279, NK280, NK282, NK318, NK323, NK394, NK395, NK397, NK405, NK406, NK419, NK422, NK423, NK425, NK429, NK434, NK452, NK453, NK458, NK485, NK513
Fourth batch, a single VIP aircraft delivered on 31 August 1945	NK515

The Shah disembarks from his private Avro Anson Mk.XII. Despite the aircraft being fitted with a VIP interior for private use of the Shah, he ordered that it retain the machine gun turret, so the aircraft could be used for military operations when needed. (IIAF monthly)

One of the 48 Avro 652A Anson Mk.Is delivered to the IIAF as a reward for Iran's war efforts and contribution to the Allied victory. They were extensively used in the Azerbaijan crisis as a bomber, reconnaissance and transport aircraft. (War Records-12349)

RAF Crashes in Iran 1941–1943

It is important to note that during the years of the Second World War, with the British forces dominant in Iran, the Royal Air Force suffered many accidents. The following incidents are officially recorded in the archives of the RAF Middle East Command.

On 25 and 26 August 1941 two Vickers Valentia aircraft were lost during the Allied invasion of Iran. K3611 of No. 31 Squadron on 25 August 1941 and K6366 of No. 244 Squadron on 26 August 1941.

On 8 June 1943 Bristol Blenheim Mk.V, AZ998 of No. 244 Squadron, No. 119 MU, crashed near the village of Abe-barik, some 45km west of the city of Sanandaj, province of Kurdistan, Iran. Cause of crash is unknown. Crew of four, pilot Warrant Officer Class I John Evans Cosford (R/87409), leading aircraftman Archibald Crichton (987275), wireless operator Sergeant Robert Williams Fitzsimmons (1379404) and Corporal William Lavin (1000747) died and were buried in Tehran's military cemetery.

On 18 January 1943 in a flight from Tehran, Iran, to Habbaniya Communications Flight, Iraq, Lockheed Hudson Mk.VI, EW969, set out for Habbaniya but failed to arrive. The missing Hudson's wreckage was located six days later by members of the Persian Cavalry in the Karaqhan Dagh Mountains, some 180 miles southwest of Tehran. Five crewmembers and seven non-air force passengers onboard died and were buried at Tehran's military cemetery. The crew onboard were pilot, Squadron Leader George Ewart Milnes, age 29, commander of the communications flight, Stanley Ellis, Herbert Pilling, Robert Ritchie, and Rae Medina. The passengers were General Ebrahim Arfaa, Colonel Ghahremani, Colonel Sheibani, Colonel Afghami, Group Captain Greenlaw, British Air Attaché in Tehran, Mr. Stephan Childs, Director of Public Relations Bureau in Tehran and Captain Yale, of British GHQ in Baghdad.

On 24 December 1943 Supermarine Spitfire Mk.VIII, JF807 of 152 Squadron, crashed in the Persian Gulf due to engine failure. The unknown pilot was lost at sea.

On 30 January 1943 RAF Hawker Hurricane Mk.IIB, BE698, coded C, of 74th Squadron, was lost. The exact location in Iran and the cause of crash is unknown. Pilot Sergeant Robert Waugh, age 21, was killed and buried in Iran.

RAF No 74 Squadron Hurricane Mk.IICs at Mehrabad, Tehran. Eventually 10 of their aircraft were transferred to the IIAF. (Bob Cossey)

7

HURRICANES AT LAST!

Just at the beginning of the Second World War, two ex-RAF aircraft, fitted with temporary tropical filters, were selected to be ferried to Iran via Cairo and Damascus. These were Hurricane Mk.Is P3270 and P4450. P4450 was a reconditioned aircraft that first flew on 18 May 1940. P3270 was first flown in Iranian colours on 16 May 1940, at Brooklands, UK. In the end, only P3270 was shipped and received Iranian serial 2-52. The aircraft had previously served with No. 3 Squadron Royal Australian Air Force and No. 229 and No. 274 Squadrons RAF and was later refitted with the new tropical air filter developed for the Mk.IIC.[1]

As previously described, due to their own increase in aircraft demand, the British Air Ministry suspended the Iranian Hurricane order of 16 aircraft in December 1940. The remaining aircraft were instead delivered to the Indian Air Force.

With Reza Shah's known sentiments toward the Germans, and to prevent his shift toward the Axis, the British quickly decided to build the remaining 16 Hurricanes at the Shahbaz State Factory. Raw materials and finished parts were ordered in March 1941, but again, the shipment was held up citing the strong German presence in Iran as the main reason. In June, it was decided to send components for 12 Hurricane Mk.I with Merlin-XX engines. This was mainly done to keep technical advisor Frank Knight, and 11 other British staff employed at the Shahbaz factory.

With new tensions building up between the British government and Reza Shah regarding the expulsion of all Germans from Iran, the export license for the 16 Hurricanes for Iran was finally withdrawn on 15 August. This seemed to be the end of the Iranian Hurricanes.

However, after the end of the Second World War, the Allies recognised Iran's immense assistance to their cause by providing ports, railroads, and military facilities as part of the Persian Corridor. In addition, the Shah had declared war on Germany on 9 September 1943 and thus Iran had officially joined the Allies.

As a result, Great Britain, with the approval of the United States, reactivated the incomplete 1939 contract for Hurricanes in November 1943. Sixteen ex-RAF Hurricane Mk.IICs (out of the original 30), mostly in fair condition, were finally approved for delivery. As a stopgap until the delivery of the 16 aircraft in the contract, it was agreed to transfer 10 Hurricane Mk.IICs from No. 74 Squadron RAF stationed in Iran. An overview of the serial numbers of No. 74 Squadron Hurricanes possibly delivered to the IIAF is given in Table 19.[2]

Table 19: No. 74 Squadron Hurricanes possibly selected for delivery to the IIAF

Serial	Code	Serial	Code
Z4144	F	BN371	
Z4944		BP284	
Z4958	Z	BP342	
BA131	Y	BP664	
BE226	F	BP708	
BE336	D	BP932	C
BE698	C	DG624	
BG904		DW932	C
BH233	Y	HL564	
BM624	A	HV660	
BM664	B	HW294	
BM968	X		

Hawker Hurricane Mk.IIC, serial 2-13, equipped with a tropical filter and plugged wing cannons, delivered as trainer to the IIAF. (RAF Hendon)

A commemorative photo of RAF No. 74 Squadron personnel at Mehrabad airport, Iran. Noteworthy is the Indian guard at far left, instead of an Iranian guard. (RAF photo gallery)

Other RAF Hurricane squadrons such as Nos. 123, 127 and 237 were also stationed in Iran between September 1942 and April 1944, but no documents exist to confirm that any of them provided aircraft to Iran.

In November 1943, Hawker Aircraft Sales Manager F.H.M. Lloyd visited Tehran. He assembled and trained a group of Iranian technicians, aided by a small team of Hawker and Rolls-Royce personnel, to prepare the assembly of the Hurricane Mk.IICs destined for Iran. However, the delivery schedule slipped until after the end of the Second World War. In August 1945, finally Iran received the long overdue 16 Hurricane Mk.IICs. They were given as compensation for the confiscation of the nine Curtiss Hawk 75A-9 planes and the use of the Shahbaz State Factory after the 1941 invasion of Iran by the Allies.

The Hurricane Mk.IICs were powered by 1,460hp Rolls-Royce Merlin XXII inline engines. However, some of their four Hispano Mk.I/II cannons were removed and replaced by stub fairings to maintain the centre of gravity of the aircraft. Since the aircraft were

Following the end of the Second World War, Iran finally received 16 Hurricane Mk.IICs as compensation for unfulfilled orders, war damages due to the 1941 invasion, Iran's assistance during Persian Corridor, and for the use of the Shahbaz State factory by the RAF. (Dmitri Kessel)

purchased to perform as monoplane fighters, it can be questioned who gave the order to remove the aircraft's guns, as they could now only be used in the advanced training role.

Iranian Hurricanes wore the standard RAF North African desert sand and dark brown camouflage with light blue undersides. Like most of the other British aircraft serving in the Middle East these aircraft had red spinners. Their serials were believed to range from 2-01 to 2-32 with the '2' prefix identifying the type to be a trainer.

Despite their official designation as advanced trainers, they were also used as bombers, armed with four 250lb or two 500lb bombs. It is not known if any of the Iranian Hurricanes ever received the '3' prefix, used for fighters. There is pictorial evidence that Iranian serials include 2-03, 2-09, 2-13, 2-18, 2-22, 2-26, 2-31, and 2-32.

The Iranian Hurricanes formed the 1st Fighter Regiment, which included the Operational Training Unit (OTU) at Ghaleh Morghi and 2nd Fighter-Bomber Squadron based at Dowshan Tappeh air bases. Immediately after delivery, training started by two RAF instructor pilots at Ghaleh Morghi of 28 ex-Hawker Hind pilots selected for the Hurricane squadrons. Old logbooks show an average of eight to 13 hours of training per month per pilot.

Two single-seat Hurricanes were lost when they crashed during the 1951 Iranian air race. In addition, four Hurricanes were damaged during the Azerbaijan and Kurdistan conflicts by ground fire, one was repaired and the other three were used as sources of engines and spare parts. The last Hurricane in Iranian service, serial 2-13, was withdrawn from service in March 1955. It is believed most of the Hurricanes were scrapped in Tehran between 1955 and 1958.

TWO-SEAT HURRICANES FOR THE IIAF

In addition to the 26 single-seat Hurricanes, two two-seat Hurricane TMk.IICs were also supplied to Iran. This variant was a unique modification and aside from another single example of a two-seater supplied to the Soviet air force, no other two-seater Hurricane trainer has ever been built for the RAF, or in fact for the air force of any other country. These were ex-RAF Mk.IIBs, KZ232 and KZ236, fitted with tropical air filters and an additional cockpit to the rear.

The conversion was simple, and no major undertaking was required to add the second cockpit with both designed as open cockpits initially. The conversion of these aircraft was undertaken by drawings prepared in 1940 to develop a trainer as a replacement for the Miles Master and T-6 Harvard, but the project was abandoned by the RAF in 1940 before the aircraft was built.

The aircraft could be flown from both cockpits, with the instructor in the rear cockpit and the trainee in the front. The rear seat was fitted with a rudimentary set of controls for the instructor and all of the radio equipment was deleted to compensate for the weight of the second pilot. The second cockpit was positioned aft of the existing cockpit without extensive modification to the structure. The top fuselage stringers were terminated about 4ft. (1.20m) further aft and additional cross members being inserted between the longerons.

The first aircraft, with Iranian serial 2-31, was initially flown on 27 September 1946 by Hawker test pilot Bill Humble from Longley with its four 20mm Oerlikon cannons retained for stability trials. The aircraft underwent conversion to include Mk.IIC wings and was transferred to the Airplane & Armaments Experimental Establishment (A&AEE) at Boscombe Down on 2 April.

Additional tests revealed that the transparent fairing between the cockpits for shielding the rear open cockpit generated considerable discomfort for the instructor in a very draughty cockpit from the air flow turbulence caused by the various screens and fairings in front. Therefore, additional stringers were added aft of the rear cockpit together with a sliding canopy taken from a Hawker Tempest with a windscreen. Eventually, both aircraft 2-31 and 2-32 were delivered with their cockpits enclosed.

The two-seat Hurricane trainers, along with four Hawker Hinds and three dual-control Hawker Audaxes were used by the IIAF's Advanced Flying School at Tehran's Mehrabad airfield, which had produced 108 fighter pilots between 1941 and 1947.

Sadly, KZ232 crashed during a training flight near Kahrizak, south of Tehran in 1949, killing both pilots, Captain Jahangiri and Cadet Moshiri. The other two-seater, KZ236, was damaged in a landing accident in 1951 and was scrapped in 1954.

Persia (Iran) ordered Hurricane Is in 1939, which were flight tested and delivered in May 1940 but the war prevented further arrivals. In 1946, the country ordered 16 reconditioned ex-RAF Mk.IIc variants for use as advanced fighter trainers. Additionally, a pair were converted into two-seat trainers. The first of these was 2-31, which was first flown on September 27, 1946. Initially both had open cockpits - 2-32 illustrated. HAWKER

The two Iranian Hurricane TMk.IIC two-seat trainers, 2-31 and 2-32 were modified single-seat Mk.IIBs. Their non-camouflaged bare metal finish with light white overcoat distinguished them as trainers. Serial 2-32 is illustrated with both cockpits open and wing cannons plugged. (Hawker)

Hawker Hurricane TMk.IIC, 2-31 during a test flight with both cockpits open. Note the four wing-mounted cannons retained for stability tests. (Aeroplane)

Hurricane 2-31 after it was fitted with a bubble canopy from a Hawker Tempest. Eventually the front cockpit was also enclosed with the Hurricane's standard canopy. (Air Pictorial)

The Young Shah Flies

The economic aftermath of the Second World War, including the occupation of Iran in 1941 and the excessive use of resources during the existence of the Persian Corridor, had weakened the Iranian economy and armed forces. More specifically, the air force was at its lowest level in terms of number of aircraft, personnel and combat readiness.

To ensure Iran's siding with Allies, Britain suggested Reza Shah abdicate in favour of his son Mohammad Reza, ensuring his position as the new king of Iran. Reza Shah stepped down and was sent to exile at Mauritius and later to Johannesburg, South Africa. On 16 September 1941 Mohammad Reza was sworn as the new King of Pahlavi.

The 22-year-old shah embarked on a massive programme to elevate public morale and to rebuild the military. To encourage young Iranians to join the military, more specifically the air force, he decided to take flight training courses.

On 22 May 1946 his pilot training started on Tiger Moth 109 with his instructor Colonel Majid Bagheri at Dowshan Tappeh airbase. After 33 hours and 18 minutes of training, he made his first solo flight on Tiger Moth 158 on 23 June 1946. He received his flying wings on 23 September 1946 from the oldest Iranian pilot, Major General Ahmad Nakhjivan. With his passion for aviation, he quickly advanced his flying skills and within a few months he flew the Hawker Hurricane and Avro Anson during the Azerbaijan conflict.

In later years he qualified solo in many other types of aircraft and was able to fly most of his personal aircraft. These included the Vickers Viscount, Boeing 707, Fokker F27, MS-760 Paris and Lockheed Jetstar. He also flew many types of helicopters such as the HH-43, AB-205, AB-206, AB-212 and Sikorsky S-61.

On 23 September 1946, Major General Ahmad Nakhjivan, the oldest Iranian pilot, pins flying wings on Shah Mohammad Reza after his first solo flight. (Aseman Iran)

Shah Mohammad Reza in the rear cockpit of a DH.82 Tiger Moth during his pilot training. (IIAF monthly)

The Shah poses in full IIAF uniform in front of a Hurricane at Mehrabad airbase. The presence of wing guns suggests that the Hurricane must be one of the ex-RAF No. 74 Squadron aircraft passed on to the IIAF. (IIAF archive)

THE AZERBAIJAN CRISIS

After the Allied invasion, Tehran's Ghaleh Morghi airbase came under the control of the Soviets and the Dowshan Tappeh airbase, where the Shahbaz State Aircraft Factory was located, was taken over by the Royal Air Force. In 1942, the Isfahan air units were distributed to Ghaleh Morghi, Shiraz, and Kermanshah. By 1943 only one wing consisting of two fighter squadrons remained at Isfahan.

After the end of the Second World War, the Hurricanes entered service with the 1st Regiment at Ghaleh Morghi in 1946. During their introduction to the IIAF service, their aircraft were baptised in combat when the Azerbaijan crises erupted.

A few months earlier in November 1945, the Autonomous Republic of Azerbaijan, led by Soviet protégé Jafar Pishevari and supported by Iran's Tudeh Communist Party, declared an independent state in the north-western part of the country, with the city of Tabriz as its capital. The short-lived state existed between November 1945 to December 1946.

In a similar move in neighbouring Kurdistan, the Kurdish separatists led by Qazi Mohammad who was supported by the Barzani tribes living in Iraq, established the Kurdish Republic of Mahabad. Both Autonomous Republics enjoyed the support of the Soviet Union.

According to the treaty signed between Iran and the Allies during the 1941 invasion, the foreign forces guaranteed their complete withdrawal from Iran immediately after the end of the war. In accordance with the treaty, British and American troops evacuated Iran in 1945. However, the Soviets refused to leave and instead they supported both revolts.

Under the orders of Shah Mohammad Reza, infantry and armour units of the army were deployed to both disputed provinces. However, in support of the separatist uprisings, the remaining Soviet troops in Iran blocked the federal forces from entering Azerbaijan, Khorasan, Kurdistan, Gorgan, Mazandaran, and Gilan provinces.

The Shah ordered the air force to support the army. As the only capable fighter-bomber in the Iranian air force inventory, Hurricanes played a decisive role in support of the ground forces. With no cannons for strafing, they flew bombing missions by dropping 250lb and 500lb bombs on enemy columns and escorted infantry and armoured columns of the ground forces. When the hostilities broke out, Iranian pilots had minimal experience on the newly delivered Hurricanes. Despite this, they were able to provide close air support to the ground forces, which helped to push back the Azeri forces in Mianeh, Ardabil, Mahabad, Khoi, Maragheh, Miandoab, Zanjan, Saqqiz and Tabriz.

As mentioned above, the Shah was a keen pilot himself. Having recently qualified on the Hurricane, he flew several reconnaissance missions over enemy forces to assess their size, location and movements. The photographs taken by his modified Hurricane Mk.IIC – equipped with a F24 (5x5 inch) camera fitted to its port side wing cannon compartment – helped to precisely locate rebel positions for artillery counterattacks by the army.

According to Iranian National Archive documents, the Shah flew 36 combat sorties in Hurricane and Anson aircraft logging 86 hours flying time in the course of three weeks. The close air support and bombing missions executed by Iranian Hurricanes and Hinds eventually pushed the Kurdish tribes led by Qazi Mohammad back into Iraq. The separatist forces of the Azerbaijan Democratic Party surrendered to the federal army led by General Zahedi.

The Azerbaijan crisis officially ended when the Iranian army, led by Brigadier General Mir Hossein Hashemi, entered and recaptured Tabriz, the centre of the East Azerbaijan province. Jafar Pishevari fled to the Soviet Union. The military organisation of the Tudeh Party was officially dissolved and its head, Abdolsamad Kambakhsh, a dismissed Air Force officer, also fled to the Soviet Union.

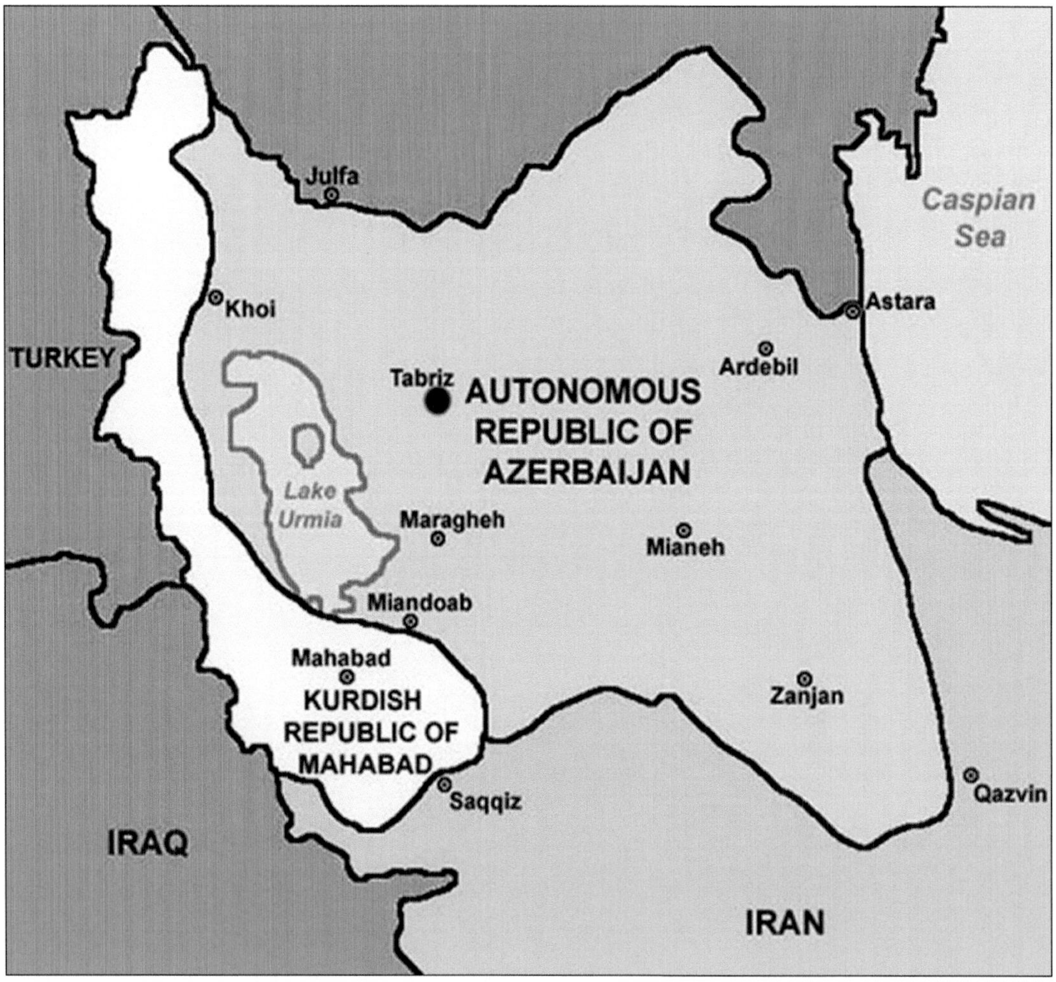

The two short-lived rebellious republics of 1945–1947: the Autonomous Republic of Azerbaijan and the Kurdish Republic of Mahabad.

An IIAF Hawker Hurricane escorts an army convoy deploying forces to Mianeh during the Azerbaijan crisis. Despite the lack of machine guns, the Hurricanes' presence flying top cover over army units was a deterrent to enemy attacks. (Doug Tidy)

With fewer than 30 hours flying solo on the Tiger Moth, the Shah started to fly Hurricanes to evaluate and photograph the Azeri and Kurdish separatist positions. His Hurricane was uniquely fitted with a camera inside the wing cannon compartment. (Aseman Iran)

The Shah gets into his Hurricane at Mehrabad for a reconnaissance flight over Azerbijan. Note the unidentified Bristol 170 unloading a truck in the background. (IIAF archive)

An Attempt at a Rebel Air Force

During the Azerbaijan crisis, the People's Democratic Front tried to form its own air force. The Tudeh Party's military branch was led by discharged pilot officer Abdolsamad Kambakhsh who assigned high-ranking Tudeh Party member Lieutenant Colonel Mohammad Bagher Agehi as the commander of the planned air force. In order to get aircraft for this new air force, he invited disgruntled IIAF pilots to join the new air force and deliver hijacked airplanes to Tabriz. Some volunteers showed up.

On 20 February 1946, 1st Flight Lieutenant Javad Zarineh and his mechanic Sergeant Mohammad Ali Peyda stole a Hawker Hind from Ghaleh Morghi and flew towards Tabriz. However, he landed in a swampy area near the Shibli pass, some 60km south of Tabriz, when his aircraft ran out of fuel. The aircraft sustained damage during landing and became useless due to the lack of spare parts and repair facilities in the newly declared autonomous republic.

On 13 April 1946, 1st Flight Lieutenant Morteza Zarbakht and 2nd Flight Lieutenant Ali Judi hijacked two Pegasus-powered Hawker Audax biplanes from Dowshan Tappeh and flew towards Azerbaijan. Both aircraft were devoid of machine gun ammunition or bombs. This flight became known as 'the Flight to Freedom' in Tudeh Party publications.

In May, both aircraft made flights over Tabriz, dropping leaflets announcing their escape and encouraging people to join the Free Azerbaijan Air Force. They expected more officers to follow, but that did not happen.

Two days after the liberation of Zanjan on 23 November 1946, the Shah, at the controls of Anson 704 flew to Zanjan and ordered a large portion of air force aircraft to be deployed to Zanjan to secure the city to prevent any possible return of separatist forces. The first aircraft, Hawker Hind 609, landed the next day. The deployment continued for the next three days, with the arrival of close to 80 aircraft of various types at Zanjan airport by the end of November.

Through the airlift established between Tehran and Zanjan, personnel and considerable volume of military and humanitarian supplies were transported by Avro Ansons to the liberated cities throughout Azerbaijan, while several De Havilland DH.82 Tiger Moths were flying as light utility, communications and observation aircraft in support of the airlift.

Despite the victory of the armed forces, the Shah continued to fly his observation flights with Avro Ansons, one such flight was on 6 December 1946 in the company of Major General Razmara. During this flight over the Ghaflankooh elevations of the Sahand Mountains, the last remaining base of the separatists in the area was discovered and reported to Army Headquarters. On 8 December 1946, an Avro Anson piloted by 1st Lieutenant Masih and Lieutenant Farhang, with Major Zehdi as observer, was sent to bomb the area. During their return at 800 metres altitude their Avro Anson was hit by heavy ground fire, but the crew managed to return the damaged aircraft to Zanjan for a safe landing. After the liberation of Tabriz on 11 December 1946, an independent air regiment was re-established at Tabriz under the command of Major Ezazi (later General).

During the Kurdistan conflict, Avro Ansons were also active, flying out of Hamadan airport. From this airfield, they carried out bombing and reconnaissance missions against the Mahabad Democratic Party of Kurdistan in the Dehe-Kord and Abe-Barik regions. With the effective backing of the air force, the Mahabad Democratic Front collapsed on 15 December 1946 and federal forces entered and captured Mahabad the following day. On 14 March 1947, federal forces seized total control of the East and West Azerbaijan provinces, finally ending the Azerbaijan and Kurdistan crisis.

THE REVIVAL OF THE IIAF

By 1947, after the Azerbaijan crisis ended, Soviet and British influence in Iranian military affairs started to diminish further when Iran and the United States signed an agreement on the Military Aid Program (MAP) and the establishment of the US military advisory mission (ARMISH-MAAG) to assist in training the Iranian army.

In the fall of 1948, Major General Razmara, the Chief of Army Staff, decided to disband the IIAF, and use its personnel to form two armoured battalions. At that time, the Iranian Air Force had 488 personnel on staff, including 47 fighter pilots and 65 operational aircraft.

Razmara ordered Air Force Major Mosvar Rahmani to prepare and present the plan for the dissolution of the Air Force within 48 hours. While presenting the plan to Razmara, Major Mosvar Rahmani convinced him not to implement his decision and instead think about reviving the Air Force. As a result, Razmara appointed Colonel Mehdi Sepahpour as the chief-of-staff and Major Mosvar Rahmani as chief of operations of the IIAF.

While the study was carried out by the Air Force staff, it was found that Iran, with its sheer size and thousands of miles of borders, needed 450 airplanes. However, due to the lack of skilled manpower, the force could not absorb more than 150.

During the Shah's visit to the United States in 1949, he met with President Harry Truman. The Shah requested the delivery of 120 aircraft to Iran. The US government approved his request and would provide him this number of planes from the surplus stocks. These aircraft would be supplied to Iran via the Military Aid Program (MAP). The American era of the IIAF had begun.

Avro Anson 707 (foreground) and 705 of the 1st Bomber Regiment at Dowshan Tappeh's hangar #6 during maintenance. (AKTA)

BIBLIOGRAPHY

DOCUMENTS & ARCHIVES

AELR – (Air & Espace – Lucht- en Ruimtevaart) – Brussels Air Museum, Belgium
Arkhiv Voyennoy Aviatsii (Military Aviation Archive) (in Russian)
British National Archives
British War Records
Douglas Aircraft
Farokh Foundation (in Farsi)
Flight Digital Archive
Fondation Francaise de L'aviation (in French)
French Historic Aviation Society (in French)
French National archives (in French)
Hawker Aircraft
Historica Fandom (in Spanish)
IIAF Association (in Farsi)
IIAF Museum (in Farsi & English)
Imperial Aeroclub Association (in Farsi)
Imperial Iranian Air Force-IIAF archive (in Farsi)
Imperial Iranian Air Force Museum (in Farsi & English)
Imperial Iranian Army archive (in Farsi)
Iran Civil Aviation Authorities (in Farsi & English)
Iran Ministry of Road and Transportation (in Farsi)
Iran Planning and Budget Organisation (in Farsi)
Iran Zamin Data Centre (in Farsi)
Iran-e-Ghadim (in Farsi)
Iranian Historic Society (in Farsi)
Iranian Marking Database (in Farsi)
Iranian Ministry of Oil and Gas (in Farsi & English)
Iranian National Archive – Digital (in Farsi)
Iranian National Archive – Stats
Iranian Post and Telegram (in Farsi)
Nemadin Foundation (in Farsi)
Narodowe Archiwum Cyfrowe (in Polish)
Pahlavi Foundation (in Farsi)
Pahlavi National Library (in Farsi & English)
Persian Civil War archive (in Farsi)
Persian Junkers Company archive (in Farsi, English & German)
RAF – 74 Squadron documents
RAF – Personnel database
RAF Hendon Museum photo archive
Soviet Heritage Foundation (in Russian & English)
The Museum of Flight
Turk Hava Kuvetleri (Turkish Air Force) (in Turkish & English)
Turk Havacilik Aylik (Turkish Aviation Monthly) (in Turkish)
Turk Havacilik Tarihi (Turkish Aviation heritage) (in Turkish & English)
U.S. Army
U.S. National Archives
War Ministry of Iran – Level2, (in Farsi)
World War One archives
World War Two archives
Yesil Bursa Tayyaresi (Green Bursa Aircraft) (in Turkish)

BOOKS

Breguet, Emmanual, *Breguet - Un siècle d'aviation* [Breguet – a century of aviation] (Privat, 2012) (in French)
Crawford, Alex, *The Hart Aeroplane AP1404A (Air Publication)* (HMSO Air Ministry, 1932)
Crawford, Alex, *Hawker Fury and Nimrod* (Casemate Publishers, 2007)
Cuny, Jean and Raymond Danel, *French Combat Aircraft 1925-2005* (Docavia, 2006)
Davilla, James and Arthur Soltan, *French aircraft of the First World War* (Flying Machines Press, 1997)
Dean, Francis H., *Curtiss Fighter Aircraft: A Photographic History - 1917-1948* (Schiffer Military, 2006)
Fereydoon, Lt. Gen. Jahanshah, *Farmandehan-e-Nezami Iran* [Military Commanders of Iran] (Pacoima, CA, USA: Ketab Corporation, 1985) (in Farsi)
Grey (Ed.), C.G., *Jane's All The World Aircraft – 1919-1938* (Sampson Low, Marston & Co Ltd., London, various years)
Green, William, *Observer's Book of Aircraft 1942-1961* (Frederick Warne, 1962)
Gunston, Bill, *Aircraft of World War One* (Octopus Books, 1984)
Gunston, Bill, *Aircraft of World War Two* (St. Michael/Octopus Books, 1982)
Jahan, Capt. Farazmoradi, *Nabard Dar-Aseman – vol. 1 to 3* [Combat in the Air] (Sepah House of Books, 1998) (in Farsi)
Kay, Anthony L., *Junkers Aircraft – 1919-1945* (Putnam Aeronautical Books, 1971)
Jones, Geoff, *History of Douglas DC-3/C-47 - 80 Glorious Years* (Fonthill Media, 2015)
Léonard, Herbert, *Chasseurs Russes et Soviétiques - 1915-1950* [Russian and Soviet Fighters – 1915-1950] (ETIA, 2009) (in French)
Léonard, Herbert, *Les chasseurs Polikarpov* [Polikarpov fighters] (Editions Larivière, 2004) (in French)
Listemann, Phil H., *Hawker Fury (Part 1)* (Philedition, 2015)
Listemann, Phil H., *Hawker Fury (Part 2)* (Philedition, 2015)
Maslov, Mikhail, *The King of Fighters: Nikolay Polikarpov and His Aircraft Designs: The Biplane Era* (Warwick: Helion, 2020)
Mason, Francis K., *The Hawker Audax & Hardy. Profile Publications Number 140* (Leatherhead: Profile Publications, 1965)
Mason, Francis K., *The Hawker Fury. Profile Publications Number 18* (Leatherhead: Profile Publications, 1966)
Moshiri, Ziaedin and Bahram Meshgin, *Az Keykavoos Ta Aryamehr* [From Keykavoos to Aryamehr] (Negin Publishing House, 1961) (in Farsi)
Moss, Peter W., *The de Havilland Rapide. Profile Publications Number 144* (Leatherhead: Profile Publications, 1966)
Robertson, Bruce, *British Military Aircraft Serials 1912-1963* (Ian Allan, 1964)
Salam, Bahrame, *Asemane Iran* [Iranian Sky] (Imperial Aeroclub, 1971) (in Farsi)
Sohrab, Kianfar, *Forughe-Javedan* [Eternal Light] (Pars Publishing, 1953) (in Farsi)
Talebzadeh, Aryan, Hamid Fardoost and Rayan Baharmast, *The 4000 Year History of the Army of Iran: From the Elamite Civilization to 1941, the Iran-Iraq War* (Tehran: Entesharat-e Iman, 2002) (in Farsi)
Tolouyi, Col., *Tarikhe Niroye Havyee Shahanshahi* [History of IIAF] (IIAF Headquarters, 1975) (in Farsi)
Turner, Eugene L., *The Fabulous 30s* (Zuber, 1959)

Walters, Brian, *Junkers: Ein Pionier der Luftfahrt* [Junkers: A Pioneer of Aviation] (Sutton, 2016) (in German)
Wilkins, Mark C., *Spad Fighters: The Spad A.2 to XVI in World War I - Legends of Warfare* (Schiffer Military History, 2019)

PHOTO COLLECTIONS

Anderson, Lennart
Buckingham
Comas, Matthieu
Dmitri Kessel
Farrokh, Keyvan
Jackson, A.J.
Gerow, Russell T.
Grothe, Will
Russian Heritage
Yadegarhaye Tehran

WEBSITES

aerospacetalk.ir (in Farsi)
Airbattle.ru (in Russian)
Airpower
Airwar.ru (in Russian)
artiklar.z-bok.se (in Swedish)
armyhistory.org/the-persian-gulf-command-and-the-lend-lease-mission-to-the-soviet-union-during-world-war-ii
defensemedianetwork.com/stories/lend-lease-to-russia-the-persian-corridor
FSU.edu
Ganj-e-Jang (in Farsi)
iiaf.net (in Farsi & English)
iranmilitaryforum (in Farsi & English)
Iranviation.com (in Farsi)
JangeJahaniDovomiranpictorial (in Farsi)
myaviation.ir (in Farsi)
Network54
parstimes.com/history/persian_gulf_command/corridor4
Pond5
webdoc.sub.gwdg.de/ebook/p/2005/CMH_2/www.army.mil/cmh-pg/books/70-7/70-7_09.htm
wehrmacht-history.com (in German)
WW2 Stats

INDIVIDUAL CONTRIBUTIONS

Atayee, Behruz
Atrvash, Abbas
Behmanesh, Fereydoon
Bohme, Adolf
Cooper, Tom
Cossey, Bob
Elsaker, Paul van den
Farrokh, Kaveh
Gray, Charles
Guston, Phil
Kares, Marcel
Kessel, Dmitri
Khosravinejad, Mehdi
Koos, Volker
Lambert-Moller, Fredrik
Lotniczy, Przegląd
Lucierre, Jaque
Matofi
Mirpanj
Nassirkhani, Fred
Ortega, Pizo - SNA
Ott, Gunther
Peeters, Sander
Riahi, Sohrab
Salem, Captain Jahangir
Sepahbody, Lieutenant General
Stewart/AB-IX
Stuart - DH Moth Club
Sims, Charles
Taghvaee, Babak
Tidy, Doug
Yoxall, John

MAGAZINES

Aeroplane
Aeroplane-Profile series
Air Enthusiast
Air International
Air Pictorial
Air War Pictorial
AirFan, in French
Airplane
Aircraft Illustrated
Amniate-Parvaz (IIAF Safety Buletin) (in Farsi)
Armée de l'Air (in French)
Aseman-e-Iran (in Farsi)
Aviation
Aviation Focal
Aviation Review
Flug Review (in German)
Flugwelt (in German)
Flying Review
Hava-Faza (Air & Space) (in Farsi)
Historia de la Guerra (in Spanish)
IIAF Monthly (in Farsi)
Interavia (multi-lingual)
Iranian Aviation Review
L'Aeronatique (in French)
L'Avion (in Farsi)
Parandegan [Birds] (in Farsi)
Sanaye Nezami (in Farsi)
WW1 airwarfare (in Farsi)

NEWSPAPERS

Entesharat-e Iman [Faith Publishing], Tehran (in Farsi)
Etelaat [Information] (in Farsi)
Keyhan [Cosmos] (in Farsi)
Mardom [People] (in Farsi)
Motafeghin [Allies] (in Farsi & English)
Pravda [Truth] (in Russian)
Sherafat [Honor] (in Farsi)
Sobhe-Emruz [This Morning] (in Farsi)

ENDNOTES

Chapter 1

1 The PS-2 was a Soviet-built F 13, manufactured by Polikarpov at its Fili plant near Moscow. Fili-built F 13s were called JU-13 while PS-2 was their Soviet designation. They were powered by the Junkers L-2 engine.

2 The four aircraft included two older BMW-III-powered F 13a variants with a shorter fuselage and razor-shaped tail, and two newer Jupiter powered F 13f variants with a 1.6 metre longer fuselage, modified wings and landing gear and a squared-off tail.

3 When CH-130 landed at Istanbul, Turkey, to change its floats to landing gear, it was confiscated by the Turkish government due to incomplete paperwork for requesting permission to land and fly over Turkish territory.

Chapter 2

1 The PAAC remained an integral part of the army under command of the Army chief-of-staff, until February 1955, when the Imperial Iranian Air Force (IIAF) was separated from the Army and formed as an independent branch of the armed forces.

2 Not S.42 which is widely mentioned erroneously in publications.

Chapter 3

1 Pilots Ahmad Khosravani, Yadolah Azam Zangane, Mahmoud Khosravani and Mahmoud Ghaem-Maghami arrived before the fifth cadet, observer Khalil Marjan, returned from the Istres flying school in 1929. With the return of five more pilots from the Soviet Union in 1929 (Bayat Makouee, Masoud Diba, Afshartous, Sepahpoor, and Hossein Haghee) the Persian Army Air Corps now had 28 pilots, observers and mechanics on hand.

2 These Soviet pilots were Colonel Andrei Kuzmin, Lieutenant Vladimir Petrov, 2nd Lieutenant Dimm Kovalenko and 1st Lieutenant Ivan Koprofiev, who flew the route with stops at Volgograd, Grozny, Baku, Anzali and Qazvin.

3 Leningrad was formerly known as Petrograd. It was renamed in 1924.

4 The airmen were Captain Ahmad Khosravani, 1st LieutenantYaddolah Azam Zangane, 2nd Lieutenant Mahmoud Khosravani, 2nd Lieutenant Mahmoud Ghaem-Maghami, 1st Lieutenant Khalil Marjan, 2nd Lieutenant Mahammad Jahanshahi and 2nd Lieutenant Afshartous

5 The six Persians were Colonel Ahmad Nakhjivan, 2nd Lieutenant Issa Khan Shtodakh, 1st Lieutenant Mehdigholi Ghahremani, 1st Lieutenant Fatollah Zand Ansari, 2nd Lieutenant Hossein Haghee and Captain Ebrahim Makouee.

Chapter 5

1 The N2C-1 was selected for the US Navy after an evaluation that was part of a competition with 14 other submissions. The first of 51 N2C-1s and N2C-2s was delivered to the US Navy in 1928. The Fledgling was a conventional biplane design with two-bay, staggered wings of equal span braced with N-struts and a fixed tailskid undercarriage. The pilot and instructor sat in tandem open cockpits.

2 Curtiss delivered seven N2C-1 kits to Turkey in 1933, as part of an agreement to produce the Curtiss Hawk Model 35 under license by the local Kayseri Airplane factory (KTF). They entered service in 1933 at the Hava Okulu (Flying School) as trainers for observers and gunners.

3 The Praga E.114, first flown in 1934 was a high-wing, cantilever monoplane seating two in a side-by-side cabin. The E.114 was an all-wood aircraft with a two-spar, single piece wing. The spars and ribs were built from pine and plywood, and the wing was covered by plywood. The wing section was flexed at the trailing edge. The wing had a constant chord centre section with a taper on the trailing edge outboard and rounded tips. The ailerons were plywood covered and unbalanced. Its fuselage was a pine framed, plywood covered hexagonal box, with the straight edged fin an integral part. The rudder was rounded and horn balanced. Though the rudder was wood framed and covered, the tailplane, mounted just above the fuselage and externally braced from below, had a tube steel structure and was fabric covered. The elevators were balanced by an elastic rope to the control column. Later, after the transfer of the E.114 to the air force, the EP-ACA registration was reassigned to a Rearwin 8125 Cloudster of the Imperial Aeroclub.

4 The RWD-13 prototype was constructed using parts from a broken up RWD-6, but its construction was more similar to the newer RWD-9. Its prototype, registered SP-AOA, first flew on 15 January 1935. Since the RWD-13 was not supposed to be a competitive plane, the main differences from the RWD-9 were an inline engine with lower power output instead of a radial engine, and simpler wing mechanisation. It still had advantages over the RWD-9, such as short take-off/landing runs and ease of flying along with good stability. By 1939, some 85 were produced. The aircraft was a three-seat, strutted high-wing monoplane of mixed construction. The fuselage consisted of a canvas-covered metal frame and an engine section covered with aluminium sheet. The Two-spar rectangular wing of wooden construction was covered with canvas and plywood in front.

The wings could be folded rearwards and were equipped with automatic slats. The empennage was a cantilever design, covered with plywood on the stabilisers and canvas on the rudder and elevators. The aircraft contained a closed cabin with three seats with two front seats fitted with dual controls and behind them a third seat and a space for luggage. The cabin had a pair of doors. The 130hp Walter Major 4, PZIn2. four-cylinder air-cooled inverted straight engine was a licensed-built copy of the de Havilland Gipsy Major. The propeller was a two-blade wooden Szomanski with a fixed pitch. The landing gear was conventional with a rear skid. The fuel tanks were in the wings with a capacity of 140 litres. Fuel consumption of the aircraft was 28 litres/hour.

5 In 1944 Iran became a member of International Civil Aviation Organization (ICAO) and was assigned the EP (Empire Persian) prefix.

6 Aside from the three Rapides mentioned, one more standard DH.89B, owned by Airwork, registered G-ADCL (c/n 6277), and 11 more Dragon Rapides had been operated in Iran since 1934 for the Anglo-Iranian Oil Company. G-ADCL was transferred to the Spanish Nationalist Air Force in 1938 and became 40-1, replacing the original 40-1 (G-ADYK c/n 6310) lost in battle.

7 To secure an order, Spitfire Mk.I N3169 was flown from Malta to Tehran for demonstration and evaluation. The type was accepted by Iran and an order for 24 Spitfire Mk.Is was placed. The start of the Second World War in September 1939 and the RAF need for fighter aircraft prevented the delivery of any Spitfires to Iran.

8 It was only after the end of the Second World War that the British government approved the delivery of 16 Hawker Hurricane Mk.IICs equipped with tropical filters.

9 During the Azerbaijan crisis, Oxfords were used to regularly transport personnel and deliver supplies to the front at Mianeh, Ardabil and Shahre-Kord. Its secondary task was air ambulance, evacuating the wounded from the battle zone to provincial centres for treatment.

Chapter 6

1 The Anglo-Persian Oil Company (APOC) was renamed Anglo-Iranian Oil Company (AIOC) in 1935.

2 No. 11 Squadron RAF and its aircraft were transferred to the RAF Far East Command in Singapore nine days after they first flew over Iran. No. 11 Squadron operated both Vincents and Blenheims simultaneously whilst based in Iraq.

3 Bandar meaning port.

Chapter 7

1 In serial books, P3270 is also listed as missing in France, struck off charge on 18 August 1940, while serving with No 501 Squadron. However, since no data or further details are known, it cannot be established as its confirmed final fate. In addition, Iranian military documents report that P3270 crashed in an uncontrollable spin at low level near Tehran's Mehrabad airport on 3 June 1951, during the famous Imperial Aeroclub air race, killing its pilot, Lieutenant Eftekhari.

2 When No. 74 Squadron RAF moved from the UK to Egypt they had no aircraft, as they were lost at sea during transit. Being informed that they would receive 24 brand-new Supermarine Spitfires by the time they moved to Shaibah, they received 28 Hurricane Mk.IICs instead. No 74 Squadron moved to Iran with its Hurricanes in 1942, initially based at Tehran's Dowshan Tappeh airbase from October to December, later moving to Mehrabad air base from December 1942 to May 1943. In March, the squadron moved to Abadan, and after a short stay they moved to Habbaniya in Iraq permanently.

ABOUT THE AUTHORS

Leon Manouchehrians, born in Tehran in 1950 to Armenian parents, dedicated his life to studying Iranian civil and military aviation. By 24, he was contributing to the Imperial Iranian Air Force's publishing department. After moving to the US in 1978, he launched *Iranian Aviation Review* magazine and later authored *Illustrated Directory of Civil Aircraft of Iran*. He lives in Glendale, California.

Sander Peeters was born in Dubai, UAE in 1978 to Dutch expats and lived in the Persian Gulf region up to 1983. He returned to work in Saudi Arabia and the UAE between 2005 and 2012. With his interest in aviation and history, he supports Leon's work by copyediting his articles for the *Iranian Aviation Review* magazine. He lives in Alberta, Canada with his wife and two children.